SUPER SUCCESS

Philip Holden

SUPER SUCCESS

Discover your true potential and get what you want out of life!

PIATKUS

First published in Great Britain in 1996 by
Judy Piatkus (Publishers) Ltd, 5 Windmill Street, London W1P 1HF

The moral right of the author has been asserted

A catalogue record of this book is available from the British Library

ISBN 0 7499 1483 1

Edited by Pamela Dix
Designed by Chris Warner

Typeset by Action Typesetting Limited, Gloucester
Printed and bound in Great Britain by
Mackays of Chatham PLC, Chatham, Kent

To Ann, Emma and Alice

CONTENTS

Acknowledgements

I would like to thank Andrew Hunter for his research work, Loretta Rolston for her typing, Allan Kinross for his support, and everybody at Piatkus for their help. Most of all, thanks to Ann, who is the best editor and wife in the world!

Grateful thanks to these publishers and authors for permission to use copyright material:

BBC Worldwide – B. Lynch, *BBC Health Check* (1989).
BBC Books – G. Hargreaves, D. Morfett & G. Bown, *Making Time* (1993).
BBC Education – P. Davies & P. Hodson, *Tomorrow the World: Develop Your Confidence* (1991).
A.C. Batsford – I. Rosenwater, *Sir Donald Bradman* (1978).
Sphere Books – D. Shipman, *Marlon Brando* (1989).
Good Housekeeping Magazine – S. Toksvig, 'Look Who's Talking' (January 1994).
Sidgwick & Jackson – R. Heller, *The Supermanagers* (1984).
Harper San Francisco – D. Hanson Bourke, *The Sleep Management Plan* (1990).
HarperCollins – D. Fingleton, *Kiri* (1982); D. Lessing, *African Laughter* (1992).
Reed Consumer Books – J. Lyle, *Understanding Body Language* (1993).
Nicholas Brealey – J. Mole, *Mind Your Manners: Managing Business Cultures in Europe* (1995).
Little, Brown – N. Major, *Joan Sutherland* (1987).
Curtis Brown Group – E. Hillary, *Nothing Venture, Nothing Win* (1975).
Reader's Digest Magazine – R. Keiner, *The Rebirth of Anthony Hopkins* (December 1992); T. Veres, *What I Learned from Raoul Wallenberg* (February 1993); T. Bouquet, *Winning By A Smile* (December 1993);

Personal Glimpses (July 1993), G. Perret, *How To Get A Laugh* (February 1992).

Weidenfeld & Nicolson – A. Walker, *Elizabeth* (1990).

Bantam Press – N. Schwarzkopf and P. Petre, *It Doesn't Take a Hero* (1992).

INTRODUCTION: IMPROVE YOURSELF!

YOUR FUTURE is in your hands. You can shape it into a success or a failure: the choice is yours. You and you alone, must accept responsibility for your future happiness. No one else can do it for you. You must improve and make the most of yourself, which does not necessarily mean being the best, although trying won't do you any harm! Your success depends on making the most of your potential.

But what does this mean? **Striving to become the best possible human being.** This emphasises the importance of stretching yourself to the limit without breaking: challenge without stress. But challenging yourself for what purpose? To help you answer this question, think of all the different roles you play every day: spouse, parent, son or daughter, employee, friend, charity worker, community helper. This book aims to help you improve in all these different aspects of your life. The danger in this highly competitive world is forgetting that our job is only one – albeit important – facet of our lives. We forget that **the quality of our lives is dependent on our relationships with others.** Human beings are social animals: they can't survive satisfactorily without love and the companionship of other people.

I love life and I want you to do the same! This is why I wrote this book. My life hasn't always been a bed of roses, but love has consistently pulled me through. My wife and two small daughters have brought real purpose to my life and hope for the future. I have always put family before money, a philosophy that has given me endless joy. A smile from them is priceless and worth everything to me. So balance between work and family is an important priority. But it hasn't always been like this. Before I met my wife, Ann, I was a workaholic and work dominated my life. I was my job, and so I couldn't put my work into perspective. I missed a reassuring voice saying that it wasn't as important as I thought.

I became prone to stress, both at work and at home. My effectiveness and creativity suffered, because I failed to give myself enough time to relax and unwind. But I have learned that it is possible to do better work in less time, if you are mentally and physically refreshed. The demands of my family mean that I must use my limited work time to the full. In fact, I have been at my most creative in the years following the birth of my children despite the sleepless nights!

You, too, must make time for yourself and take control of your life, if you are to achieve super success and happiness. Give yourself time to be yourself. Reflect on your situation, decide what's right for you, and then act accordingly. Renew yourself with continual lifelong learning and a passion for self-fulfilment.

A crucial element in my success has been my relentless will to win. I have never been content with second best and have always sought to excel in everything. Successful people think they are special and capable of changing themselves and the world for the better. So this book's message is that **success comes from within you**. You must be aware of your responsibilities not only to others but also to yourself. As the psychoanalyst Carl Jung once pointed out, to love somebody you must first love yourself. You must have the dignity and self-esteem that comes from living a useful life. But don't let your loved ones suffer because of your pursuit of career success. You are more than your job, you are a human being with a life outside your work.

Striking a balance between your work and leisure is clearly very important in fulfilling your potential. A life without time for your loved ones is a life wasted, and your work will be less fulfilling if it does not allow you time to love. Section A of this book will help you to find that time with the people who really matter to you, and so make the most of yourself. Success comes first of all from self-motivation, the will to live for excellence and to do great things in your life. If you are to be truly happy, such a desire must be directed to achievement in its widest sense – doing useful things inside and outside work. This is the subject of Chapter One.

However, self-motivation isn't enough. You also need the confidence and assertiveness to defend your right to be treated with humanity and respect. There is nothing wrong, of course, with being 'nice' – far from it. Much joy and happiness in life comes from cheerfully giving to other people. But don't be a doormat. You will lose respect if you haven't got the courage to say 'no' sometimes. Chapters Two and Three will show you how to do this, and be a good person without being manipulated and exploited. They will discuss the importance of thinking positively – a 'can do' mentality.

Confidence is also an essential prerequisite of making the most of your mind, which is looked at in Chapters Four and Five. Their central theme is simple: **brain power is learning power**. You must be a lifelong learner and realise that learning does not stop when you leave school or university. Look, listen and learn from your mistakes every minute of your life. A love of learning will smooth your path to the other mind improvers discussed in these chapters: creative thinking and problem solving skills. You will receive practical advice on how to improve both of these.

The biggest enemy of learning is time – or to be more precise, the lack of it. People seem to be too busy to reflect and invest in their relationships with others. Chapter Six helps you solve this dilemma by discussing time management techniques. You can make room for both work and leisure by making better use of your time. Be fanatical about not wasting it and think about the quality of your time by asking yourself, 'How can I achieve my goals as quickly as possible?'

Time is life itself, but without a healthy and stress-free life we have nothing. There seems to be so much conflicting medical advice at the moment. Butter or margarine? Alcohol or no alcohol? Chapter Seven helps you to sort out this maze and give you the energy to do the things you want to do in your life. There is more agreement among doctors than you may think. One thing in particular they are agreed on is how stress contributes to many physical and psychological illnesses, and Chapter Eight shows how to control stress in your life. In particular it tells you how to find peace of mind in a turbulent world. Never forget that all the money in the world won't automatically give you that calmness and security which only comes from spiritual contentment. Look into your soul for the seeds of a happy life.

Another vital factor in psychological well-being is how effectively we deal with other people at work. This is discussed in Section B of the book. Chapter Nine looks at how to improve your oral and written communication skills. To communicate with confidence and influence, you must win respect, make people your friends, be a good team player, and learn to sell and negotiate. These are all discussed in Chapter Ten.

Chapter Eleven discusses how to become a great manager, with the central message that today's manager must be 'tough but tender' – tough and courageous enough to make difficult decisions, but caring enough to win respect and inspire people to do great things. This ideal manager is no longer a supervisor and controller, but a coach and facilitator. Motivating people in this way is essential to your organisation providing the best possible service to its customers. How this can be done is discussed in Chapter Twelve. Remember: no customers, no organisation, no job!

There may come a time in your life when you want to get out of the rut you are in and find a career which will give you the fun and fulfilment lacking from your present job. You may even have no job at all. Section C has been written for all of you! Chapter Thirteen looks at how you can really love your work, and Chapter Fourteen concentrates on one particular way of doing this – setting up your own business. More and more people are becoming self-employed, and one of them could be you.

Section D looks at the eight recurring themes of *Super Success*: fulfilment, love, courage, freedom, fun, hope, life-long learning and self-marketing. If you can successfully apply all these to your life, you will surely make the most of your potential. Great people in the past have done it and you can, too!

This book is filled with examples of people who have found the path to success and fulfilment. Their spirit of humanity and hope has helped them to win through. Follow their example and listen to the advice and the ideas that inspired them. My intention in this book is to help you learn from every relevant subject – in particular, philosophy, psychology and history. By opening your mind to every possible source of knowledge, you will be able to understand yourself and other people better. This is the path to success.

So read on and take the advice of one of Anthony Robbins' books: *Awaken the Giant Within You!*

1

THE WILL TO WIN: MOTIVATE YOURSELF TO SUCCESS

This chapter will show you how to:

▶ *Identify your needs*

▶ *Set realistic goals*

▶ *Motivate yourself to achieve those goals with passion, enthusiasm, and excitement*

▶ *Think your way to success using techniques such as visualisation*

THE YEAR WAS 1992. The place was Barcelona. The man was Linford Christie. In under ten explosive seconds, he achieved his lifetime ambition of the Olympic gold. Christie said afterwards, 'Success is not simply a matter of

1

being fast or strong. What it's really about is being tough mentally. To get to the top you've got to have guts, determination and a hard, hard attitude.' This is what this chapter is all about. It will show you how to succeed through a will to win. It will make you a self-starter who gets up every morning – including Mondays – and does something positive and constructive. You can do this in seven ways:

Self-motivator No 1: Understand What Your Needs Are

What exactly are your needs likely to be? Abraham Maslow, an American psychologist, provided an answer to this question. Work out which are the most important for you by ranking them in order of importance:

- *Physiological needs* Hunger, thirst, sex and shelter.
- *Safety needs* Security and protection from both physical and psychological loss.
- *Belongingness and love needs* Acceptance, friendship, affection, sense of being part of a group, to love and be loved, to like and be liked.
- *Esteem needs* Self-esteem, power, prestige, esteem from others, achievement, self-confidence, independence and freedom.
- *Self-actualisation needs* Personal fulfilment. Realising one's full potential as a productive, creative person. The need for purpose and meaning in life.
- *Cognitive needs* The desire to know and understand, including aesthetic needs (a need for the beautiful).

In short, your needs are either largely physical – related to your body – or spiritual – concerned with your soul. They are both important, if you are to be happy and successful. Ask yourself: what is the purpose in your life? Who are the people who are most important to you and are you doing everything you can to make them happy? Surely there is no point in having a successful career if this means having an unhappy personal life. So striking the right balance between your work and leisure is crucial to understanding your needs.

Self-motivator No 2: Find Goals Which Inspire You

Rupert Murdoch is one of the most self-motivated people in the world. He says he is driven by ideas and power, and that power gives him the chance to leave the world a better place. Money is also important to him, but only as a means of expanding his business empire and ensuring his family can live well enough. With five homes, including a mansion in Beverly Hills and a yacht, his family needn't worry!

So Murdoch is motivated by setting himself inspirational goals. To do the same you must make sure your goals are challenging but realistic – be ambitious, but don't strive for the impossible. And you must have the support of your loved ones. If they don't care about your aims in life you will start to have doubts about how worthwhile these aims are. So make sure your family is right behind you! Encourage them and other people to give you regular feedback on how well you are achieving your goals, but your goals must not conflict with your values and satisfying your needs.

Here is a step-by-step guide which will enable you to set yourself inspirational goals:

STEP 1: DEFINE YOUR LIFE'S PURPOSE

This may seem like asking you to re-write *War and Peace*, but it must be done. Have a broad philosophy which constantly influences your behaviour and the more specific goals which you set yourself. A one-line personal mission statement can be a great help here, like: 'Put family first'; 'Pursue a passion for spiritual purity'; 'Show compassion for others', 'Live usefully'. Think up your own and do it right now!

STEP 2: ANALYSE YOUR NEEDS

Re-read the list of six needs at the start of this chapter, and reflect on the importance you placed on them.

STEP 3: THINK OF THE PEOPLE WHO REALLY MATTER TO YOU

You must, of course, think of yourself, but pure selfishness won't give you lasting happiness. This comes from your relationships with other people. Remember that unhappy relationships will leave holes in your life which all the money in the world won't be able to fill.

STEP 4: IDENTIFY YOUR INSPIRATIONAL GOALS

Thinking about your life's purpose, needs and loved ones will enable you to identify specific goals. These are some examples:

- Move mountains for your spouse and children.
- Put others before yourself.
- Value time, not money.
- Be a lifelong learner.
- Make your work fun and fulfilling.
- Stand up for what you think is right.
- Stay healthy.
- Take control of your life.

Make sure that you do all that you can to achieve these goals. If you don't, you'll regret it.

Self-motivator No 3:
Never Give Up

Best selling authoress Barbara Taylor Bradford wrote four unpublished books before she hit the big time with *A Woman of Substance*. She wanted to be a writer more than anything else and her steely determination saw her through to fame and fortune. Behind every successs story like hers there are countless failures and disappointments. So don't view failure as a disaster from which you will never recover, but as a stepping stone on the road to success. Learning from your mistakes is the important thing. British comedian Les Dawson said just before he died that he achieved success through knowing failure. Doctor Scott Peck started his best selling book, *The Road Less Travelled*, with the words 'Life is difficult', a philosophy based upon the first Noble Truth of Buddhism. Don't expect that your life will always be easy. Success won't be delivered to you on a plate. So be positive and optimistic in the face of your difficulties – see life as a challenge which puts obstacles in your way occasionally. Don't be daunted by them, but have faith in your ability to overcome them.

Never let that optimism be destroyed by bitterness. The obvious reaction in times of distress is 'Why me?', but such questioning is self-destructive. Try and accept what has happened to you as quickly as possible and then get on with your life. Make your life easier by rewarding yourself for your successes. Let yourself enjoy the successes which you work so hard to achieve, think about what you have achieved, and pat yourself on the back for it. Don't concentrate on the things that you didn't do. This is why perfectionists are often dissatisfied. Strive for high standards, but don't pull yourself apart in the process. Eleanor Roosevelt, wife of the former President of the United States, once summed up her philosophy by saying, 'I can feel it in me sometimes that I can do much more than I am doing, and I mean to try until I do succeed'. If you have the same perseverance, you won't go far wrong.

Self-motivator No 4:
Think Success

He was the son of a baker in South Wales and was a total failure at school. His classmates decided he was dim-witted 'Mad Hopkins'. But Anthony Hopkins went on to become an Oscar-winning actor. Why? From his self-doubt as a boy grew an iron determination to prove his critics wrong. He now says, 'In spite of my insecurity, I always believed I was destined for some kind of greatness'. Against all odds, you, too, can have a rendezvous with destiny, if you believe you can do something well. There are several things you can do to 'think success':

- *Visualise your success* Sit down and think about what you want to do successfully. See it in your mind, as if it was a real experience, and really concentrate on it. You are better able to visualise successfully if you are relaxed. So do a few relaxation techniques beforehand (see page 83). Megastars have been using visualisation to improve their performance for years. Golf supremo Jack Nicklaus always made sure that he 'saw' the ball being hit near the hole, before actually hitting it. Arnold Schwarzenegger has said, 'As long as the mind can envision the fact that you can do something, you can ...' So why don't you do the same?
- *Talk success to yourself* Before something you want to do well in, work up some passion and enthusiasm by talking to yourself. Say things like: 'I can do this.' 'I am going to show those so-and-so's.' 'My idea is a good one, and I'm going to show them that it is.' 'I can be a success.' 'I will be what I want to be.' Such positive thinking can really give you the confidence to succeed. Avoid negative thoughts like 'I can't do this because ...' Acknowledge

your successes. Don't wait for someone to praise your work – do it yourself!

● ***Don't build obstacles in your mind*** When you are striving to do something difficult, it is so easy to make excuses for laziness. 'I haven't got the time because I'm so busy.' 'I can't do this because I'm always so tired.' Make an effort, and then you will see that thinking about doing something is much worse than actually doing it. I regularly got up at 5am to write this book, even with a full-time job and two babies to look after. It can be done, if you put your mind to it. Instead of criticising you, your loved ones will love you even more for doing something worthwhile.

● ***Be motivated by the fear of failure*** Use such anxieties positively by saying to yourself things like, 'I know this is difficult, but I can do it if I try like mad'. You must make sure that your anxiety doesn't turn into crippling self-doubt. Avoid thoughts such as 'I'll end up regretting my decision'. Your biggest regret will be missing a great opportunity in your life.

● ***Don't fear success and purposely fail*** Success can be feared for a number of reasons. You may see it as a threat to your personal relationships, or to some desirable characteristic. Some women fear high achievement because they regard it as unfeminine and a danger to their role within the family. You may also feel unworthy of success and lack the confidence to sustain it. Beware of such negative thinking – success needn't be a threat. Remember that you can achieve things in any aspect of your life, not just a job. You can be successful without a successful career, if you believe that what you do outside paid employment is useful and worthwhile.

Self-motivator No 5:
Have a Cool Head But a Warm Heart

Think again about your purpose in life. Research shows that happy people have happy relationships, so feeling compassion, empathy and responsibility for others is in your own interests as well as theirs. Be motivated by people – do it for your loved ones! Feel responsibility for them, and then you will move mountains for them, just like Raoul Wallenberg, a Swedish diplomat in the Second World War who courageously saved thousands of Jews in Budapest during the Nazi occupation. He was motivated by a belief in the worth of each individual human being. Wallenberg was an ordinary person who was driven to an extraordinary life through his compassion for others.

A warm heart isn't enough, however. You also need the mental resilience to make the really tough decisions. For example, a philosophy of helping others is all very well but whom do you help? If you give your time to one person, you can't give it to someone else. Therefore you will have to be decisive and make priorities. The rights and wrongs of a decision may not be clear-cut either. You may have to choose between two things which are right, or the lesser of two evils. As we shall see in Chapter Eleven, one of the ethical dilemmas facing managers today is the need to make people redundant to ensure the long-term survival of their organisation. In these circumstances you must have the emotional detachment to be decisive. It may be necessary to be cruel to a few employees to protect the jobs of the rest of the workforce.

Self-motivator No 6:
Live for Excellence

Fred Astaire was the greatest dancer ever in the movies. He could generate romance simply by floating around on the dance floor. 'I make love with my feet,' he once said. But behind his success was an incredible capacity for hard work and an obsessive desire to be number one. Great performers in other professions have this same obsessiveness, like golfer Nick Faldo, who has made his hands bleed through putting practice. They live for excellence. How you can do this is the main theme of this book. But four particular ways to live for excellence can be mentioned here:

- *Compete with yourself not with others* Worrying about how other people are doing might discourage you and distract you from the most important task of all – improving your own performance.
- *Value what you are striving for* If you believe that your goals are worthwhile, achieving them will be easier and more rewarding. Do something that makes you feel good.
- *Remember time past is gone for ever* What greater motivation could there be than using your time for the benefit of others? Be driven by the desire to make the most of every moment and the thought that every day might be your last. Don't waste your life.
- *Be ruthlessly self-disciplined* Make sure you have the right attitude. Be prepared to give up anything in your pursuit of success. Get your mind and body in shape, so that you can effectively drive the road to excellence. Be special, and avoid mediocrity like the plague.

Self-motivator No 7: Love Life!

'To succeed you have to believe in something with such a passion that it becomes a reality,' as the Body Shop chief executive Anita Roddick once said. You must love everything that you do. You must have a reason to get up in the morning. You need passion, enthusiasm, and excitement in your life. Let's finish this chapter by looking at the ten golden rules for a happy and passionate life based upon current research. Some of these rules will be expanded upon further in other parts of the book.

The 10 Golden Rules of Happiness

1 **Have the Right Values**
   Have the courage to do what you think is right.
2 **Love Somebody**
   Relationships with others are the most important cause of happiness. Excite others and they will excite you!
3 **Hold on to Your Dreams**
   To be happy you must have purpose and set challenging goals.
4 **Fulfil Your Dreams**
   Persevere to achieve your goals.
5 **Find Peace of Mind**
   This can be done through:

   a Oneness With Yourself i.e. total harmony between body and soul.
   b Accept The Past, Live For Today and Look To The Future.
   c Freedom of Spirit – take control of your life.

6 **Money**
   This gives security and status, but don't be enslaved by it. Use it to do other things.
7 **Stay Healthy**
   Find ways of improving your physical fitness to give yourself more energy.
8 **Find the Right Balance Between Your Work and Leisure**
   Don't let your work sacrifice your family and friends.
9 **Have a Good Laugh**
   Laugh at yourself as well as with other people.
10 **Use and Develop Your Talents To The Full**
   Make the most of what you've got.

One Final Comment

You will never succeed in life if you are not self-motivated. A will to win will enable you to do things you might have thought impossible. 'Man alone can perform the impossible,' as the American philosopher Ralph Waldo Emerson once wrote.

2

BOOST YOUR SELF-CONFIDENCE

This chapter will show you how to:

▶ *Boost your self-confidence*

▶ *Improve your self-image*

THIS CHAPTER will show you how to increase your confidence in what you do and how to relate to other people. You need the self-belief to have the courage, faith and self-reliance to become a success. Indeed one of the most important messages of this chapter is that confidence comes from purpose, a belief that what you are doing is directed to some worthwhile activity. It is that inner resolve which will help you to take on the world and become a winner. This is what helped the Australian Sir Donald Bradman to become the greatest batsman the world of cricket has ever seen. His self-confidence came not only from his natural talent but also from enormous self-discipline and an indomitable will. Such application made him a sporting colossus, but it was his wife Jessie whose support helped to sustain that success, and keep his feet firmly on the ground. 'There have been times when without her I would have found it impossible to carry on,' he once said. Indeed Bradman was a great man as well as a great cricketer. His integrity and high ethical standards meant that his confidence was never undermined by a loss of self-respect. You, too, can have the same confidence if you remember the seven key points of this chapter.

Confidence Booster 1:
Be Assertive

If you are assertive, you are able effectively to defend your rights as a human being. In particular you have the right to be treated with respect and to say 'no' to people. (The next chapter will give you ten tips to become more assertive.)

Confidence Booster 2:
Fill Yourself with Pride

There is no better way to feel confident and optimistic for the future than having pride in your performance. Such pride comes from purpose, a faith and belief in what you are doing. So find that purpose by defining your goals clearly and make sure that they touch your heart and your mind.

Purpose isn't enough, though. Pride also comes from excelling at something, even if it is something very small. It might just be doing the washing up, or giving your partner breakfast in bed. But whatever you do, do it really well. As Nigel Mansell said after winning the world motor racing championship: 'I don't believe in luck. You have to work hard for success.' The confidence he exudes is testimony to this conscientiousness, even though he faces the possibility of death around every corner. To do this yourself, you must keep control over your emotions, and if you're going to do something badly, don't do it. Singer Elaine Page once received this advice from Dustin Hoffman: 'Never audition when you're not in control.' So Page refused to do the audition for *Evita* when she had 'flu, even though her agent urged her to go.

Confidence Booster 3:
Improve your Self-image

How do you view yourself – with satisfaction or desperation? There is no point in looking at yourself in the mirror and cursing yourself for your weaknesses. You will only get bitter and you won't improve. Instead do something positive about your self-image by following these six tips:

- *Know yourself well* Understand your strengths, weaknesses and potential. Take pride in your strengths and don't belittle them. But don't be too introspective or self-conscious. Don't dwell on your deficiencies – be positive and try to put them right. Identify when you feel most and least confident during a day and analyse the reasons why.

- *Look after your appearance* You feel as you look. See page 101 for how you can dress for success.

- *Have a thick skin* Don't worry about what other people say – stick to your guns!

- *Don't hijack your honour* Be true to yourself. Don't forget your values and your loved ones. Such an inspirational purpose will motivate you to look after yourself. This relentless self-discipline is present in all successful p ople.

- *Reward yourself* If you do something well, reward yourself. Don't scold yourself and think you could have done better. Think of the rewards that will most please you – talking positively to yourself, a trip out with the family, or your favourite chocolate bar! But don't over-indulge yourself, because it will make you feel guilty. Instead consider continued learning as essential to a rewarding and fulfilled life. Consequently you should even reward your failures, when you are genuinely trying to learn and succeed. Former Olympic hurdler Kriss Akabusi has said, 'You can't learn to win until you've known how to lose.' The achievement of something worthwhile is the biggest reward of all. So at the end of each day write down five things you have achieved during that day. Then read it again first thing in the morning to set you up for the day. This is a great confidence booster!

- **_Generate excitement in your life_** Having fun and excitement makes you feel good!

Confidence Booster 4: Think About Other People

You will feel confident if you make others happy and feel important. So having the right balance between your work and leisure is vitally important to your confidence. John F. Kennedy attributed his success to the attentions of his father. 'He made his children feel that they were the most important things in the world to him,' JFK once said.

Remember that your views are as valuable as anybody else's. Imagining the other person in the bath will certainly remove any superiority you might have given him or her in your mind! If that doesn't give you enough confidence, seek help from other people. Olympic gold medallist Sally Gunnell relies heavily on her coach, Bruce Longden, for her confidence to win. At seventeen she was overlooked for the Los Angeles Olympics and thought her world was at an end. Longden told her, 'Listen, you're never ever going to get left behind at home again. From now on we make sure they have to pick you.' We all need a shoulder to cry on sometimes. Going on a confidence building course may be a good idea, and meeting other people who feel the same way will give you a boost. Ask about such courses at your library or the management department of your local university. Also get personal recommendations from friends or colleagues, or go for established names in training.

Confidence Booster 5:
Conquer Your Fear and Anxiety

You have three possible reactions to difficult situations: flight, fright and fight. To be confident you must fight and conquer fear and anxiety. There are a number of 'fear fighters' you can use to do this:

- *Slow down* Adopt a 'no hurry, no worry' philosophy. Stand back and stay cool!
- *Seek support from other people* A problem shared is a problem halved. Talk openly with a good friend or professional counsellor.
- *Live one day at a time* Concern yourself only with today and don't be anxious about tomorrow.
- *Tough-mindedness* Say to yourself 'I will survive!' Have the strength and determination to overcome the problems that life throws up – violence, prejudice, bereavement, failure, the unknown, mental anguish and pain. Calmly look reality in the face, think positively and say as Franklin D. Roosevelt once did, 'The only thing we have to fear is fear itself.'
- *Beat stress* Controlling stress reduces anxiety and tension. Meditation and relaxation techniques can help a great deal. Hypnosis may also be worth a try in your fight against fear.
- *Assess the odds* Concern yourself only with things that are likely to happen.
- *Remove your guilt* Accept your past and seek forgiveness.
- *Think nice thoughts* Re-assert your control over things you are afraid of. Some people have conquered their fear of flying by learning how to fly an aeroplane themselves! You also need to learn to calm a troubled mind and banish unwanted thoughts. Keep busy to stop yourself dwelling on your problems.
- *Put things into perspective* Make sure that you

concentrate on important things. Life is too short to worry about things which in retrospect will seem trivial. In times of difficulty it is so easy to blow up a problem out of all proportion. Don't do this – treat every problem on its merits. Ask yourself: 'What is the worst that can possibly happen if I can't solve my problem?' The answer is never as bad as you fear.

- *Remember that other people are human, too* Give yourself confidence in your relationships with others by realising their failures and appealing to their humanity.
- *Get all the facts* Information gives you the power to deal with a problem better.
- *Smile, smile, smile!* Seeing the funny side of problems can ease your worries.
- *Love for others* A genuine concern for others will make you less fearful in your relationships with them. Say to yourself: 'If I care for him, why should I be afraid of him?'
- *Learn how to lose* Minimise the risks involved when you make a decision, so that any failures are not devastating to you. Learn to accept the inevitable.
- *Look at the pros and cons of doing something* If you are making a decision, write down the pros and cons on the left- and right-hand side of a sheet of paper. Compare the two lists, taking into account which points are particularly important to you. Benjamin Franklin used this technique to help him do the right thing and minimise worry – you can do the same! For example, think about changing your job. On the plus side you may be moving nearer family and friends, with promotion, more money and greater fulfilment. You may also be leaving behind an unpleasant boss or colleagues. On the minus side a promotion may mean more stress and less time to enjoy your family and leisure. Never forget that the grass often appears greener on the other side of the fence. Don't run away from problems – they might just recur in another job. So move for positive reasons.

Confidence Booster 6: Valiant Be! Have The Courage To Succeed

Great people know the importance of valour, or moral courage, in their lives, none more so than the President of South Africa, Nelson Mandela. Twenty-seven years of imprisonment did not diminish his spirit. 'I have done my duty to my people and to South Africa,' as he said in the dock in 1962. Pugnacity comes from the purpose that Mandela had.

Be positive and follow your conscience. Do your duty, accept your responsibilities, and do what you think is right. Keep resolute, even when the whole world thinks you're crazy.

Real courage comes from being aware of the consequences of your actions. Think about not only what you are doing but also why you are doing it. Admit you might be wrong sometimes, even if it means losing face. Humility is often the ultimate test of a courageous person. If this all seems a bit much for you, remember that you don't have to stand alone at the times of trial in your life. Actively seek the help and support of the people who really believe in you. They will help you to win through.

Confidence Booster 7: Think Positive

The phrase was coined by Norman Vincent Peale in his book *The Power of Positive Thinking*, first published in 1952. Since then countless successful people have used it to good effect. Take film star, Elizabeth Taylor, for example. While making a film she nearly lost the sight of one eye when a wind machine blew a small piece of metal into it. She didn't panic about something which would have ruined her career. She said at the time: 'I didn't think that I wouldn't see again … I had enough faith. I believed it would [work out all right]. If it hadn't it would have been the end of my career, but not my life.' She believed her favourite children's authoress, Frances Hodgson Burnett, in the *Secret Garden*: 'Thoughts – just mere thoughts are as powerful as electric batteries.' Here are some tips on how you can re-charge your mind to think more positively:

● ***Think to change the world***   Adopt a 'can do' mentality towards everything you do in life. Don't play yourself down. If you can't do something immediately, work out how you can. Beware of pigeon-holing yourself:

> 'I'm not a practical person' – so you don't do any DIY.
> 'It's women's work to look after the children' – so you don't.
> 'I'm a woman, and women aren't meant to do these things' – so you don't.
> 'I'm not very good at public speaking' – so you never get the practice that will help you to improve.
> 'I'm a happy and contented person' – so you never learn and set yourself ambitious goals which will make your life more interesting.
> 'I'm never going to be ill' – so you never do anything positive about improving your health.
> 'Management is men's work' – so you never do it.

If you really believe you can do something, you can overcome your preconceptions and self-doubts, and do it! Doing it is often easier than thinking about it! Dare yourself to do the difficult things which are always the most satisfying.

● ***Don't think about failure***   Believe you can be successful at anything. Automatically replace a negative thought with a positive one. Don't build obstacles in your way.
● ***Have faith in your ability***   Tap into your unused potential.
● ***Never lose hope***   Positive thinking comes from optimism for the future. So being happy and successful makes

you more positive. Remember success breeds success.

● ***Talk positively to yourself*** Dale Carnegie, in his book *How to Win Friends and Influence People*, suggested that as soon as you get up in the morning you should say to yourself, 'Every day in every way I'm getting better and better!' Repeat this to yourself throughout the day, as well as positive phrases like 'I can do it,' and 'I'll show them!'

One Final Comment

There are three things above all others which will boost your self-confidence: faith, hope and passion for your future. Most important of all, you need a worthwhile purpose which will see you through the trials and tribulations of life. Without purpose your self-confidence will wither away and die. Remember the words of Abraham Lincoln, 'Always bear in mind that your own resolution to succeed is more important than any other one thing.'

3

BE ASSERTIVE

This chapter will show you how to:

▶ *Be assertive*

▶ *Defend your rights when dealing with other people*

ATTICUS FINCH in Harper Lee's novel *To Kill A Mockingbird* was a great man. Why? He had the courage to defend his right to be compassionate and take a stand against the racists of his home town, Maycomb. So Finch defended the innocent black, Tom Robinson, despite continuous threats and abuse. He was unsuccessful, but his example and defence of Robinson brought Maycomb one step nearer to becoming a humane society. To put it another way, Finch won respect by defending his rights without infringing other people's. This is the real essence of being assertive. It requires you to express your opinions, wishes and preferences more effectively. How do you rate on this? Do you cringe when you are reminded of giving way to someone on an important matter? Do you have the word 'doormat' engraved on your mind?

This needn't happen to you! All you have to do is act upon the ten golden rules of assertiveness in this chapter. Bear in mind, though, that assertiveness isn't the same as aggression. You don't have to be pushy and aggressive to be assertive. Assertiveness is a positive way of dealing with other people. It is all about making you feel ten feet tall, so that you can take on the world and win! As Eleanor Roosevelt once said, 'No one can make you feel inferior without your consent.' Do this short quiz to find out, if you have the assertiveness to avoid such feelings of inferiority:

1 Do you find it easy to say 'No' to people?
2 Are you persistent in getting what you want?
3 Do you know your rights as a human being?
4 Can you handle abuse and criticism?
5 Are you confident when starting a conversation with someone you don't know?
6 Do you always consider *your* needs in life as well as other people's?
7 In conversation do you exploit the other person's weaknesses and avoid his or her strengths?
8 Do you practise being assertive?
9 Do you stand up for your views, principles and opinions when dealing with others?

The less you can do these things, the more difficult it will be for you to be assertive. Read on if you think you need help!

The Ten Golden Rules of Assertiveness

1 SAY NO WHEN YOU NEED TO

You don't win people's respect by saying 'Yes' all the time. They will take advantage of you and you won't have enough time for the things that really matter. There are only twenty four hours in the day, and you can't possibly do everything! So here are a few tips to help you say 'No' when it really matters:

- *Think of the harmful consequences of saying 'Yes'* Stress, less time for your leisure, lower self-esteem and so on.
- *Put your foot down with your relatives or close friends, if they are taking you for a ride* You may love them, but they have no right to use you as a doormat. If they are worth your love, they will understand

if you say no occasionally. You can't please all of the people all of the time.

- **Dilute the impact of a 'No'** Say things like:

  No, I don't want to.
  No, I feel unhappy about that.
  No, I'd prefer not to.
  No, I wouldn't like to.

- **Give reasons for your decision** 'No, I feel unhappy about this because ...' Show understanding for the problems of the person you are refusing.
- **Delay, if necessary, to think things over** 'Hold on, I'd like to think about this.' Think twice about readily agreeing to do something. Beware of phrases like 'No problem, I don't mind.'
- **Keep calm** This will help you say 'No' with calm authority. Slow, deep breathing before you speak can help.
- **Practise saying 'No' to yourself on your own** This will give you the confidence to say it more readily when you need to!

2 BE PERSISTENT

Repeat over and over again in a firm but relaxed way what it is you want, until the other person gives in, or agrees to negotiate with you. This is sometimes referred to as the broken record technique. Obviously you will have to decide the points (if any) on which you are prepared to compromise.

3 NEVER LET ANYBODY TAKE AWAY YOUR RIGHTS

As a human being, remember you have certain rights like everybody else. They are the rights to:

- Ask for what you want (realising that the other person has the right to say 'No').
- Speak up for the truth and do what you think is right.

- Choose whether or not you want to understand or know about something.
- Privacy.
- The same opportunities and treatment as everybody else.
- Be consulted over the things that really matter to you.
- Control your own life and do your own thing.
- Grow, learn and develop as a human being.
- Make mistakes and change your mind.
- Help others, if you think they need it.
- Have a happy personal life and love the people you care about to the best of your ability.

Remember they are *your* rights, and nobody else's. Fight for them, if necessary. Be a Rosa Parks, the quiet seamstress who sparked off the bus boycott led by Martin Luther King in Montgomery, Alabama in 1955. She refused to go to the back of the bus, as blacks then had to do. Parks said, 'It was a matter of dignity; I could not have faced myself and my people, if I had moved.'

4   DEAL WITH PUT-DOWNS

A put-down is a question or comment which violates one or more of your rights, outlined above. The first thing to remember when dealing with put-downs is never to react aggressively. This will make the situation even more explosive and difficult to resolve. Instead, appeal to the other person's better nature. For example, 'Come on, just because you've had a bad day, there's no need to take it out on me!' Alternatively you might say, 'You know that's wrong, can't you re-consider?'

Most of all, act quickly and decisively – don't let the other person get away with it. Deny what is said and say what you feel. Say something good about yourself and make it clear you dislike the person's behaviour. Make people aware that you recognise any hidden messages in what is being said. Some examples are given below, with the real meaning and appropriate responses.

Are you really sure about this? (*That was a damn stupid idea.*)

Yes I think it is a really great idea.

Haven't you finished the cooking yet? (*You are useless and I could do it much better and faster*).
No, but you are most welcome to finish it, while I have a rest.

We really should work better together. (*I'm OK but you're not.*)
I agree, what do you think we should do about it?

I've just got to go out for a minute. (*I'm fed up with the children and I need a drink.*)
I would prefer it if you didn't. I need some help with the children.

Are you sure you can do this job? (*You are incapable.*)
Yes, I have the ability but I'm still learning.

If I were you ... (*I know better than you.*)
With respect, I still think my solution is the best one.

You are very good, given that you have a home and two children to look after. (*You are under-performing because you are a woman.*)
I'm just as good as any man, if not better!

You won't be able to do this because you are rather stressed at the moment. (*You have a stress problem.*)
Why do you think I am stressed?

Give yourself lots of practice at dealing with put-downs, however small. Remember practice makes perfect!

5 HANDLE CRITICISM WELL

We all get criticised, but can you cope with it? Are you positive about it and turn it into a learning experience, or do you just fold up at the first whiff of criticism? Here are some tips to deal with criticism positively and more effectively:

- **Stand up for yourself** Defend your position stoically, if you think it is the right one. Be firm but fair.
- **Get all relevant information** Knowledge gives you

the ammunition to counter-attack. Be clear about the reasons why you are defending yourself.

- **Be slow to anger** Losing your cool loses the argument. It gets people's backs up, so that they ignore or become resistant to what you are saying. Of course avoid physical violence, but letting your anger out on yourself can help you keep calm. Stamping your feet or cursing under your breath can be very therapeutic.
- **Don't be passive** Being timid, apologetic and indecisive doesn't help.
- **Forgive and forget** A forgiving heart is more likely to find a solution which benefits you. Generally such a compassionate attitude wins people over.
- **Relax** Use slow breathing to calm you down.
- **Wait and listen** Wait to hear the abuse so that you can clearly understand what the other person is saying. Anyway, two people can't talk at the same time.
- **Accept criticism if it is valid** There is no point in burying your head in the sand. Accept the possibility that you may be wrong.
- **Actively seek constructive criticism** Don't avoid it, because it helps you to learn.
- **Don't take unfair criticism to heart** Keep busy to keep your mind off it, and don't lie awake worrying about it.
- **Use body language to your advantage** Keep your back straight and look your critic straight in the eye.

6   KNOW HOW TO MAKE CONFIDENT CONVERSATION

The general rule to follow is to find out the person's work and leisure interests and then show a genuine enthusiasm for them, even if they bore you. Smile as much as you can and look the person in the eye. Don't put yourself down, and avoid tag phrases like 'you know' and 'OK?' Don't apologise excessively, act childishly and helplessly, giggle nervously or cry excessively. Maintain good eye contact and body posture, and accept compliments graciously.

7 THINK OF YOURSELF FOR THE SAKE OF OTHERS

You won't really love other people without loving yourself first. So assertiveness is not purely selfishness. It will give you the self-esteem and confidence to help others. But beware of false modesty and servile humility. Don't let people push you around.

8 BE SEEN NOT OBSCENE

Assertiveness is about having presence and influence. It is certainly not concerned with being aggressive which, as we saw in Point 5, is counter-productive. Anger is a different matter. Being angry and morally indignant can be used as effective motivators for becoming assertive. You need to control the anger, however, or it will turn into destructive aggression, so avoid being unnecessarily argumentative, critical, and impatient.

9 BOX CLEVER

How many times have you been duped by a salesperson at your door? Annoying, isn't it? Whoever is talking to you, take control of the conversation and get in there first. Show off your knowledge to give yourself authority. For example, 'I heard on the radio recently that what you say is wrong.' Try to keep one step ahead of the people you are talking to. Anticipate what they are thinking and going to do. Identify the weaknesses in their arguments which you can exploit. Look for any inconsistencies of argument and factual inaccuracies. Remember that the best way to find someone out is to know something about what they are talking about, or at least appear to do so!

10 PRACTISE BEING ASSERTIVE

Mentally rehearse assertive behaviour. Alternatively do it on your own or in an assertiveness training course. You can ask for details about such courses in libraries, Adult Education

Departments, and Departments of Psychology at universities.

One Final Comment

'If things are ever to move upward,' the American psychologist William James wrote at the beginning of the century, 'someone must be ready to take the first step and assume the risk of it.' Take that step to defend your rights assertively, or you will regret it for the rest of your life.

4

LIVE TO LEARN

This chapter will show you how to:
- ► *Become a lifelong learner*
- ► *Learn better*
- ► *Improve your concentration, memory and fast reading skills*

MARLON BRANDO once said of an actor, 'He must be superhuman in his endless struggle to inform himself.' Such learning means personal growth and making the most of your opportunities. Successful people believe that their education has only just begun when they leave school or university. They continually learn from their failures as well as their successes. They are fanatical in their belief that every experience is a learning opportunity, realising that to stagnate is to die. People like this love learning, because learning loves them. Research shows that it gives people happiness, fulfilment, stamina and the best possible chance of getting the job that they want. So this chapter will give you six tips to increase your learning power.

Principles of Better Learning

1 *CONCENTRATE!*

Better concentration is an obvious way to improve your learning. You can do this by making it worthwhile concentrating on something, by really loving what you're doing. It is obviously much easier to be engrossed in something which you think is fun, enjoyable and worthwhile. Think about the benefits of concentrating on something – a qualification, employability, adaptability, flexibility, sociability. Also think about the consequences of *not concentrating* – failure, less time with your family and so on. This may motivate you to learn and start an assignment as quickly as possible. Solitude and mental freshness are two other things than can help you. Find a room where you can work without interruption in an atmosphere of learning.

Make sure your mind and body are in good shape, and take as much exercise as you can. Research shows that breathing more oxygen improves the quality of your thinking. Stay fresh, because it is impossible to concentrate well if you are tired all the time. **Think about the quality – not the quantity – of your learning time.**

Evidence shows that your concentration will start to fall after about an hour of intense work activity. So take a break and work in small bursts. Get some exercise if you can, and go back to your work refreshed. But don't be distracted, and keep your work uppermost in your mind. Don't switch on the radio or TV – this will make it much harder for you to go back to your work. Watch what you eat and drink – overeating and alcohol are not conducive to concentration. Try to avoid fatty foods, as they reduce your energy levels. Remember also that it is easier to concentrate if you are relaxed and not tense or anxious. To control anxiety, deal immediately with anything that may be bothering you, and relax with slow, deep breathing.

Active listening can also help you concentrate when you are talking with other people. To do this you should consciously direct the conversation in a way which interests you. Say things like 'Something very similar to that has happened to me ...' Keep your mind active by trying to anticipate the speaker's next point. Your brain can think four to ten times faster than you can speak, so use it!

2 IMPROVE YOUR MEMORY

When was the last time you forgot something or someone's name? It is annoying and embarrassing in your relationships with other people. One professor in an American business school has over 400 MBA students, and at the start of the course he knows all of their names. It is no wonder that he has such a good relationship with them.

How can you put names to faces? One way is to do what the professor does and closely scrutinise names and photographs. Another technique is to associate a name with a particular feature of the person concerned – it can help to ask politely the derivation of the person's name, or find out some other interesting fact about the name. Also if you can, break up names and relate them to an image which is associated with the person you are trying to remember. For example, try to remember someone with the name Redford and think of that person driving a red Ford car!

The use of acronyms can be helpful – i.e. form a word from the first letter of other words. For example, the six counties of Northern Ireland (Fermanagh, Armagh, Tyrone, Londonderry, Antrim, Down) spell FAT LAD. Linking facts as well as words can also be an effective memory aid.

Consciously look for links between pieces of information given to you. It is easier to remember the completed jig-saw than all the individual pieces, after all. Putting things in classes or categories (e.g. friends, work colleagues, family) can also be helpful. Look for distinguishing features of things or people within these categories (hair colour, spectacles etc), and memorise by exception.

Another technique to help you remember words is **number word associations**. Think of a rhyming word for each number from one to ten and learn it (e.g. One, bun; two, shoe; etc). This will always be your reference point. List in numerical order the words you want to remember. For each word on this list, picture an imaginary association with your appropriate number rhyme. For example, if you wanted to remember the three words water, glass and chocolate, you could list them like this:

1 A giant *bun* filled with water.
2 A giant *shoe* made of glass.
3 A giant *tree* made of chocolate.

Notice that you remember things better in giant proportions. This principle can be extended to memorise particular events. Imagine people in unusual situations doing the things that you want to remember. The uniqueness of such situations makes them stick in your mind. For example, if you have a lunch appointment with your partner, and you have to give him (or her) some money, imagine yourselves eating on a giant raft with your tablecloth fluttering in the sea breeze and pound notes flooding down on you from the sky!

There are also ways of successfully retaining information by writing things down. Keep a little book in your pocket to write down anything you want to remember. Make lists of important things to do – shopping lists, 'must do' lists, etc. Continually re-read the key points you want to remember and then test your recall by writing or reading them aloud. Such revision should be spaced out. The first review should be about ten minutes after seeing the piece of information, the second a day later, the third a week later, the fourth a month later, and the fifth four months later. By that time it should be committed to your long-term memory. Make sure you make effective notes, so that their clarity and brevity make them easier to remember. The five principles of effective note making are:

● Be as brief as possible – the fewer words the better! There is no need for complete sentences.
● Concentrate on the key points, so selecting what's important is vital.
● Use checklists, headings, abbreviations, tables, and diagrams.

- Give yourself practice at writing faster, or learn short-hand.
- Remember that notes are to be remembered, not read out as a literary masterpiece.

People with a good memory also look after themselves. They keep their mind active. Research shows that memory can actually improve as long as the brain is used creatively and constructively. Don't drink too much, as alcohol actually kills your brain cells. Because you have billions of such cells, moderate drinking won't affect your memory permanently, but regular excess will.

3   READ FAST AND EFFECTIVELY

Readers are learners, and learners are winners. You cannot escape the fact that reading is essential to your self-improvement. This section will explain how you can do this in the quickest possible time. The good news is that you don't have to read everything! Use books of quotations – as Winston Churchill once said, 'It is a good thing for an uneducated man to read books of quotations'.

Before you pick up a book or report, be clear about what you are looking for. Use the book's index to concentrate on the particular topics that interest you. You don't have to read a complete biography to find out about someone. All you have to do is refer to the pages in the index under his (or her) name heading. Look for summaries at the start of a report, or at the end of each chapter in a book. Reading the introduction to a book can also be very informative and gives you a good overview. In a report, concentrate on the conclusions and recommendations. Only read in detail difficult or important passages of a publication – photocopy these if you can for further reference. Speed read the rest by reading the first line of each paragraph, the contents page and checklists. Your eyes should move efficiently, smoothly and methodically through the page.

A visual aid can be useful. Use a long, thin pencil to guide yourself through the words on the page. It should be moved smoothly along either *over* the line being read or *underneath* it. The pencil should be held slightly above the page. Research shows that using a pencil like this can improve your reading speed by as much as 100 per cent. It is also helpful to underline key words and phrases (provided it's not a library book, of course).

Read when your concentration and memory are at their best – avoid serious reading when you are too tired, and rest your eyes. During long reading periods, regularly look up from the book and focus on distant objects. This will relax and rest your eye muscles and save you from unnecessary fatigue. Finally, have the right posture when you are reading. This should be reasonably upright but not rigid or tense. The distance between your eyes and the book should be between 15 and 24 inches, if both your posture and desk height are right.

4   QUALITY THINKING

Always think about the *quality* of your learning. To do this remember the following points:

- *Your desk is not the only place where you can learn* Look, listen and learn all the time. Observe your environment and learn from it.
- *Stop before you're stale* Improved learning is not solely dependent on how much time you spend on it. Look upon your leisure as a learning experience in itself, and a means of re-charging your batteries for your work.
- *Learn continuously* According to the Chinese philosopher Confucius, the aim of education is constant self-improvement. Continually work on your weaknesses and build upon your strengths. There is some evidence to suggest that when you stop learning your brain starts to deteriorate. So 'use it or lose it'. Keep your brain active and challenged by reading, an engrossing hobby, or paid or voluntary work. Remember you are never too old to learn.
- *Don't underestimate your potential*   Believe you *can* learn. Don't build obstacles in your mind.
- *Use inter-disciplinary thinking* Apply knowledge

acquired in one subject area to another.

- **Practise in your mind** Mentally rehearsing a task can help you to perform it better.
- **Use technology** Technical aids such as personal computers, calculators and educational radio and TV can improve your learning. In particular, CD-ROM (a CD you place into your computer) is beginning to revolutionise learning. This will allow you to have vast amounts of information at your fingertips (books, encyclopaedias and other reference works). The computer will select for you the particular information you need. You will also be able to ask the computer questions about your subject. For example, you can now buy a computer CD with 2,000 classic books on it for just under £50.00 – 2½p a book! Another fascinating development is multimedia CD-ROM, which provides the reference information with music, photographs and flashy videos.

5   DETERMINATION THROUGH LOVE OF LEARNING

Why was the basketball superstar Michael Jordan such a great player? He loved the game and was driven by an intense competitive spirit which gave him the determination to succeed. Jordan was always testing himself in anything that he did. You, too, must have the same sort of determination if you are to learn. Learning theory (see Point 6) tells us that everyone reaches a plateau in their learning, where they temporarily find learning more difficult. Have the determination to go through that plateau and continue to learn. Don't become frustrated and give up too easily. To help you do this, seek support, positive feedback and inspiration from others. Also motivate yourself through your own inspirational goals such as a desire to make the world a better place.

6   LEARN FROM THEORY

Experts have been studying learning for years, and they have come up with the following tips to improve your learning:

- Remember the learning curve, which states that learning goes through four stages:

  1 Significant improvement in learning performance.
  2 Learning plateau – little or no improvement.
  3 Performance increases again.
  4 Improvement slows down.

  So don't be discouraged by the plateau!

- Make sure you learn at your own pace.
- Stress (pain, fear) reduces learning.
- Be motivated, learn for the rewards you get – money, compliments, etc.
- Make the learning meaningful – relate it particularly to your problems.
- Actively participate in your learning.
- Seek knowledge of results (feedback) to see how you are doing.
- Reinforce – keep on having another look at what you've learned. Give yourself ample opportunity for practice and repetition, but space out such practice.
- Remember your learning rate may be influenced by how you interact with your teacher.
- Use as many different ways as possible to learn. Use as many senses (touch, sight and sound) as you can.
- Build on previous knowledge and break down new material into logical, easy-to-follow steps.
- Proceed from the simple to the difficult.
- Learn until correct responses to situations come automatically.
- Be patient!
- Be analytical – look at the pros and cons of particular arguments and situations. Don't just describe what's happened.

7 IMPROVE YOUR PROBLEM-SOLVING SKILLS

Here are some tips to do this:

- ***Identify the problem*** It is very important to address the real causes of the problem. For example, your employees may seem to be angry about the size of a pay increase, when the root cause of their anger is the way that they are badly treated by managers. In this situation ask yourself the question: what are my people afraid of? Fear can be another important cause of problems and resistance to change. People will be particularly anxious when they are worried about losing their jobs, or their rights. See pages 23 and 24 for a list of rights which your people might consider to be important. Also be proactive – try to anticipate problems and don't just react to them. This will give you time to calmly assess possible solutions to a problem without any panic.

- **Define your objectives** Objectives will give your problem-solving purpose and direction. Make sure that you give yourself a time constraint – some problems may have to be solved very quickly. Your objectives should be challenging enough to stretch you, without being unrealistic.

- **Collect and select information** Collect and organise all the information relevant to the problem. Ask the right people the right questions. Look at everything that has been written on the subject. Don't be afraid to go outside your organisation. Suppliers, customers and libraries can all be very useful sources of information. You can also learn from the successes and failures of your competitors. But whatever you do, the most important skill is to select the pieces of information which are necessary to solve your problem. Don't swamp yourself with information so that you find it difficult to distinguish what is relevant to the problem. Focus on the key issues. Also make sure that you check your facts – information must be accurate as well as relevant.

- **Be self-motivated** Problems will be solved more quickly with the perseverance, enthusiasm, single-mindedness, and willingness to work hard which come from self-motivation. So have another look at Chapter One!

- **Look for alternative solutions** Effective problem-solving requires creative thinking. Be as original as you can, but remember that doing nothing may be the best option. Give yourself time to reflect on the problem and evaluate the pros and cons of each possible solution on the basis of the following three criteria:

Feasibility Have you enough resources effectively to apply the solution?

Suitability Does the solution use your strengths and those of your organisation? Does it avoid the impact of their weaknesses and any threats from the external environment such as the actions of your competitors? Does the proposed solution take advantage of any favourable changes in the external environment?

Acceptability Is your proposed solution acceptable to the people affected by it, e.g. other employees, customers, shareholders, suppliers, banks and the local community?

- *Think holistically* Consider *all* aspects of the problem and assess its impact not only on yourself and your department but also on your organisation as a whole. Don't forget that one problem is often interrelated to another set of problems – for example, a decision to produce a new product also creates problems in finance, marketing and personnel.
- *Seek the support and help of others* Discuss the problem with other people constructively. Remember that two heads are often better than one – small groups can usually solve problems more effectively than one person alone. People will particularly want to be involved if they think the problem is important to them. In such circumstances a consensus will have to be found. However, one person will have to take responsibility for making a decision, if decisive action is required.
- *Learn from experience* Learn from your successes and failures at work and in your personal life, and keep on doing so.
- *Be intuitive but logical* Don't ignore your intuition, but logically base your decisions on all the facts available. Akio Morita, former chairman of Sony, intuitively knew that the Walkman would be a great success, even though market research and many of his staff thought otherwise. But this was not a rash decision. It resulted from Morita's exhaustive assessment of all the available information.

One Final Thought

The English philosopher Francis Bacon once said that, 'Knowledge is power'. Become a lifelong learner and give yourself the power to set yourself alight!

5

BE CREATIVE

> *This chapter will show you how to:*
> ► *Be more creative*

WHO INVENTED or discovered the aeroplane, car, camera, electric light bulb, telephone, telescope, television, pneumatic tyre, penicillin, radio signals and radium? Answers on page 197! These were all geniuses who had the power to think creatively. But you don't have to be an Einstein to do the same – you, too, have the potential to be creative. You don't have to invent something really big, but you can creatively change the way you do things in small ways. You might cook something differently, or change the way you do your job. The key is to challenge your routine, the way you have always done things. In this chapter you will receive some tips to help you do this and become more creative, but first of all, do this self-analysis quiz.

How Creative Are You?

1 Do you actively seek constructive criticism of your new ideas?
2 Do you have confidence in your ideas?
3 Do you learn from watching things and listening to people around you?
4 Are you motivated by a worthwhile purpose in your life?

5 Do you give yourself time for reflection and relaxation?
6 Do you consistently persevere through any problems you face?
7 Do you consider yourself to be a 'free spirit' and have total control over your life?
8 Do you question things all the time?
9 Do you continuously strive to improve your learning?
10 Do you search for alternative ways of looking at a particular problem?

Finally, give yourself two minutes for each of the following questions:

11 Can you think of five different ways of using a large piece of brown paper?
12 Can you write down ten words beginning with the letter 'b'?
13 Can you think of five objects that are round, soft and edible?
14 Can you think of ten animals you would see at a zoo?

Refer to the analysis results on page 197.

Principles of Creative Thinking

1 COMMUNICATION

You can become more creative by talking with other people and even to yourself. Talking encouragingly to yourself can be a big morale booster to help you overcome any obstacles you may face on the road to creativity. Support from others can help, too. Relationships are at their most creative when there is trust, openness and communication. Lennon and McCartney worked well together in the early days because they were friends. It was only later that suspicion and mistrust destroyed their writing partnership. Listen to people and learn from them. Don't be arrogant enough to believe that you can do it all yourself. Remember your body language – if you look bored, people will be less likely to discuss their good ideas freely with you. Be genuinely interested, but don't be afraid to speak your mind when the need arises. Have confidence in your opinions. If you keep your ideas to yourself, you will never find out if they are good ones. Don't avoid conflict! Friendly disagreement can sharpen your mind and give you new ideas. Try to find the pearls in other people's minds, so that you can use them to enrich your brainpower. Creative tension with others can be very productive. Use analogies, metaphors, and a varied vocabulary to create new understandings. British Airways, for example, has found it very useful to view itself as an 'experience business' rather than just a 'travel business'.

2   RESOLUTION

To have this resolution, your creative activity must have a worthwhile purpose. It must inspire you and touch your heart. Such a purpose will arise from necessity and what you think is right. Having to do something can concentrate the mind wonderfully. 'Necessity is the mother of invention.' Another powerful motivator in creativity is the moral indignation which arises from a desire to make the world a better place. Pursue that vision with vigour, and try anything which will help you make it a reality. Here are some other tips to increase your resolve and determination:

- **Do it your way**   Have the courage of your convictions and be prepared to stand out from the crowd. But take heart – evidence shows that people are more creative when they don't get their own way.
- **Use personal tragedy as a motivator**   Ex-Beatle Paul McCartney was deeply affected by the death of his mother Mary when he was only 14 – the 'mother Mary' in the song 'Let It Be'. From that time his obsession for music became an outlet for his pent-up emotions.
- **Use your luck**   When Lady Luck comes around your corner, grab her with both hands! 'Accident is the greatest of all inventors,' as Mark Twain once said.
- **Focus on results not on activity**   What's important is

the *quality* not the quantity of time you spend on something. Don't feel that you have to be actively doing things all the time. Think, reflect and relax a bit to re-charge your mental batteries.

- **Never lose your sense of urgency** Get in first with your new idea before anybody else does!
- **Think of the rewards** Spur yourself on by occasionally thinking of the benefits you will get from your creative work – for example, money, respect, and self-esteem. Remember also that success often breeds success. Doing something well can open other doors for you.
- **Be physically fit** This will give you the energy and stamina to be creative. There is also some evidence that fitness and exercise help your imagination and clear your mind. So go for it!
- **Have a good laugh** Seeing the funny side helps to see you through the difficult times when you're not getting results. Research shows that groups are more creative if their individual members laugh and joke more.
- **Love what you do** Evidence shows that this will make you more creative. As Art Fry, the inventor of the Post-It notes once said, 'Choose the things that you like to do. You'll work hardest at it and you'll have more successes.'
- **Overcome any obstacles in your way** Highly creative people look upon any activity, whether work or leisure, as a hobby – just like Mozart (600 compositions), Thomas Edison (1,093 patents) and Napoleon Bonaparte (68 battles)! If a door slams in your face, knock it down! React to failure with steely determination.
- **Work hard** As Thomas Edison said famously: 'Genius is one per cent inspiration and ninety nine per cent perspiration.' Total dedication to the task is essential to creativity. You must eat, sleep and drink it, so that at times of relaxation (you do need them) a good idea will automatically spring to mind. If it does, write it down before you forget it. Thomas Edison used to write down his ideas in a 200-page notebook he always carried around with him. By his death he had filled 3,400 of them!

3   SPIRITUAL LIBERATION

To be creative you must be a 'free spirit', in total control of your life. But are you really free? The philosopher Hegel said that you are if you can agree with four questions. Can you do what you prefer without interference and criticism? Can you honestly say that you are not being manipulated or forced to prefer something? Are your preferences based on what you really want rather than what other people think? Do your preferences satisfy your needs?

The most important thing you can do to achieve such freedom is to make time to think and relax. Reflection and solitude are essential to the creative process. Creative people have the ability to become 'lost in the present', because they are thinking so hard. If you are given an important assignment, before you do anything else sit in a room alone with a pen and a blank piece of paper. Write down briefly all the factors which are important to this assignment and how you will deal with them. This will provide an excellent framework for more detailed action later. Ensure that you are as relaxed as possible when you are thinking. Great ideas often come when you're relaxed and least expect them. Think of Archimedes when he shouted 'Eureka' as he ran naked out of the bath.

Reflection and relaxation can give you the peace of mind which can generate the energy and enthusiasm you need to be creative. Having said this, history is littered with examples of creative geniuses with tormented souls. Beethoven is one. However, for mere mortals like ourselves, peace of mind will be a better (and happier) path to a creative life. Research shows that you don't have to be depressed, frenzied, or mad to be creative! But you do need the self-discipline and self-knowledge which both come from an inner peace.

For many people, however, the biggest obstacle to their freedom is the organisation where they work. Former American President, Harry S. Truman, referred to the White House as a prison. Do you look out through iron bars when you are at work? Avoid this incarceration by working for an organisation which actively rewards and encourages creativity. Actively seek work flexibility, because the ability to work when and where you like can be a big help to creative thinking. Ideally you should work at your most productive times (e.g. early in the morning or late at night) and in the place where you feel most creative. Where do you get your best ideas? Probably not your office because of its frenetic atmosphere and constant interruptions. Try to find somewhere more peaceful to work as much as you can. Working at home may be the answer – if you have a room to yourself and you can get away from the children! You might even be able to plan one or two days a week at home into your work schedule. If your boss wants some justification, say to him that you work better at home and so will be a more effective employee.

When you are at work, don't let meddlesome and over-bearing bureaucracy get in your way and reduce your creative thinking time. There are certain things you can do, like not volunteering to join unnecessary committees, but avoiding bureaucracy is often difficult, as Albert Einstein found. When he worked at the bureaucratic Swiss Patent Office from 1902 to 1905, the only new products he developed for them were an improved form of pop gun and a device for the control of alternating current! It was only in his free time that he had the scope to become really creative, culminating in his famous Theory of Relativity in 1905. Perhaps you may have to do something different, too, before you can be truly creative.

4 QUESTION THINGS ALL THE TIME

Leonardo Da Vinci had one of the most creative minds in history. He designed a tank, a parachute, a bicycle, contact lenses and even a water-powered alarm clock! It is surprising that he found time to paint. The roots of this genius were his passion for knowledge and his ability to question things. He was always asking the question 'why?' or 'what if?' You must do the same, if you are to be creative. So remember the following tips:

● **Challenge conventional wisdom and the status quo**
Just because people believe something is right for today
does not necessarily mean it's right for the future. Don't
be afraid to challenge those who may be threatened by
new ideas or situations. How would you have responded
to these four famous gaffes?

'Who in the hell wants to hear actors talk?' Harry
Warner, founder of Warner Brothers studios, 1927.
'I think there is a world market for about five computers,' Thomas J. Watson, founder of IBM, 1943.
'It is quite impossible that the noble organs of human
speech could be replaced by immobile, senseless
metal.' Jean Bouillaudt, member of the French
Academy of Science, talking about Thomas Edison's
phonograph, 1878.

You should hate dogma for its own sake, and beware of
blind obedience. Dogmatic thinking implies unquestion-
ing thinking. Therefore be open to new possibilities,
question every dogma and judge it on its own merits. If
it's inappropriate, reject it. Abraham Lincoln, for
example, remarked during the American Civil War that
dogma of the quiet past was inappropriate to the stormy
present. Campaigner for the blind, Helen Keller, once
wrote: 'The heresy of one age becomes the orthodoxy of
the next.' Songwriter extraordinaire Andrew Lloyd
Webber knows the wisdom of these words. He didn't
listen to his friends as a young man who said that musi-
cals like *The Sound of Music* were a 'load of rubbish'.
Instead he learned from them to produce such classics as
Jesus Christ Superstar, *Evita* and *Aspects of Love*.

● **Love failure**   In creative problem-solving, a mistake is
an experience to learn from. Don't be afraid to make
mistakes. Creative people make more mistakes than
others. As Soichiro Honda, founder of the great Japanese
corporation, once said: 'Success can only be achieved
through repeated failure and introspection. In fact
success represents the one per cent of your work which

results from the ninety nine per cent that is called failure.'

- **Seek new challenges** Once you have done something creative, don't rest on your laurels. Start thinking about your next project and look critically at your previous work. Strive to do even better the next time.
- **Avoid prejudice and superstition** Preconceived opinions and irrational beliefs are dangers to creative thinking.
- **Don't surround yourself with your opinions** Mix with people who challenge your views. Read newspapers and other publications with which you might not agree. Don't surround a false belief with other false beliefs to protect yourself from admitting your ignorance. A research study in the early 1980s found that chief executives in the USA really do this!
- **Beware of stereotyped thinking** All Italians are temperamental, all women are bad drivers, all men are insecure. Avoid thinking like this at all costs. Judge people on their merits, not by the label you give them.

5   LEARN SOMETHING NEW

St Paul wrote that you can transform your performance through the renewal of your mind. You need to continually renew your creative abilities through learning. The most important thing is never to lose a passion for new ideas. Seek variety – meet new people, do different things, because new experiences spark off new ideas. So each day make one change from your normal routine. Never stop being curious about things, because an inquisitive mind is a creative one.

Don't forget the importance of intuition and common sense either. They can open your eyes to the blindingly obvious as well as the startlingly brilliant. Scientist Stephen Hawking, when asked how his mind operates, replied, 'I work on intuition, thinking that an idea ought to be right, then I try to prove it.' Such proof can more easily come from relating the knowledge of one subject area to another – sometimes called holistic thinking. In other words, thinking in black boxes can be a serious obstacle to creativity. Research by the management writer Rosabeth Moss Kanter in her book *The Change Masters* found that cross-functional teams were the best way of promoting new ideas at work. Problems are best solved using knowledge from all relevant subjects and areas of expertise. For instance, the historical examples used in this book help to illuminate issues relating to self-improvement.

You must also learn from other people. Seek feedback from potential users of your ideas – they may highlight problems that you never knew existed. Andrew Lloyd Webber's shows are first seen privately by 160 guests, and then he invites comments. The first draft of *Aspects of Love* was virtually torn up and thrown away after a bombardment of criticism from these people. Brainstorming with other people can be another most effective way of generating new ideas. But beware of 'groupthink' – the tendency for everyone to think the same way because they are afraid of 'rocking the boat'. Management writer Robert Heller, in his book *The Supermanagers*, has these tips for effective brainstorming:

a Hold the session off the premises.
b Get yourself a round table.
c Provide facilities for visual exposition, e.g. blackboard.
d Video tape the whole session so that you can learn from the re-run.
e Hold the session first thing in the morning, for a whole morning – don't use Mondays.
f Make sure the leader is skilled and experienced in running this kind of session.
g The leader should have an aide – an assistant leader or 'facilitator'.
h Friends should not sit beside each other. The leader should sit nearest the door with the facilitator opposite.
i The number of participants (in addition to the leader and the facilitator) should be six (plus or minus one) – remember to select the right brainstormers.
j The leader must open the session by instructing the participants on how to behave – what is expected of them, and the rules of the game.

6 LOOK FOR DIFFERENT ANGLES ON PROBLEMS

This is the basis for what Edward de Bono has called lateral thinking. It aims to find entirely new ways of thinking and acting by looking at things differently. At least 25 per cent of your time should be devoted to finding better ways of doing things. Ask yourself, 'How else could I do this?' Question everything, and always ask 'Why?' Avoid thinking 'this is the way things have always been done, so it must be right'. Look at everyday situations and objects with a fresh eye. Think about water, for example, and note the number of ways you use it. The results will amaze you! Prepare yourself for the unexpected because it can be a valuable source of new ideas. Coca-Cola was invented by a pharmacist, John Pemberton, when he was looking for a headache remedy! Ask questions which throw a new light on old problems, such as: 'Why do people waste at least one fifth of their time at work? Why are certain people's views considered superior? Why do we tolerate Third World famine?'

You should consider the unlikely or the absurd by standing a problem on its head – what management writer Charles Handy calls upside down thinking. Think unreasonably. Ask yourself 'what if ...?' questions. Shape the world to *your* requirements and needs, and don't be dictated to by what other people want you to believe. For example, the Polish astronomer Copernicus, in the fifteenth century, asserted that the earth went round the sun, not vice versa as people then believed. Five examples of upside down thinking are:

Re-defining our idea of work Work should be any worthwhile activity, whether or not it is paid. Ask any housewife, househusband or charity worker!

Annual hours contracts Instead of doing the conventional 40 hours for 48 weeks a year, those 1920 hours are distributed throughout the whole year unevenly. So you could work for two months doing 80 hours a week and then have two months off.

Leisure rewards If you think that leisure is such a good thing, why shouldn't the government pay you to enjoy it?

Why shouldn't employers give you more leisure time rather than more money?

Customisation Treating every customer differently. For example, every child would be taught a curriculum especially tailored to suit his or her needs.

Work to live Put your leisure and family as your number one priority, even at the expense of your career.

One Final Thought

Make the most of your mind so that you can achieve your personal goals and change the world for the better. As Charles Handy has written in his book *The Empty Raincoat*, 'It is up to us to light our small fires in the darkness.'

6

MAKE TIME FOR
WORK AND LEISURE

This chapter will show you how to:

▶ *Use your time better*

▶ *Identify 50 ways to save time*

▶ *Get organised for success – how to be as
effective as possible at work*

▶ *Work more flexibly – how to adapt your job to
your preferred lifestyle*

DO YOU often find that you:

1 Stay late at work for an hour or more to finish something?
2 Neglect your loved ones and social life because of work?
3 Are late for important appointments?
4 Rush at the last minute to meet a deadline?
5 Set yourself unrealistic goals?
6 Concentrate on minor matters and fail to give your attention to the things that really matter?
7 Are busy but never seem to achieve much?
8 Wonder how to pack everything into a week?

If you do, your time management needs improving. So read
this chapter! Many people can't manage their time properly.
This was a conclusion of a 1993 survey of British directors
and managers carried out by the Industrial Society. It

discovered that they waste *one fifth* of their time at work. The top 15 time wasters in order of importance were:

1 Telephone interruptions.
2 People dropping by.
3 Lack of organisational planning.
4 Putting things right that were not done right the first time.
5 Poor information exchange between departments.
6 Poor listening skills of others.
7 Indecision.
8 Moving goal posts.
9 Badly organised and chaired meetings.
10 Poor management planning.
11 Unnecessary checking on others and their work.
12 Inappropriate organisation structure.
13 Overly bureaucratic office procedures.
14 Switching priorities caused by the organisation.
15 Problems with computers – 'technofailure'.

So do something about it – manage your time better and so make time for your work and leisure. Successful people are very good at doing this, by carefully selecting their priorities. TV personality David Frost has said, 'I don't like wasting money but I hate wasting time.' His success has been achieved by an obsessive will to use his time to the full.

Principles of Time Management

There are seven rules you will have to follow to manage your time better.

1 SET GOALS AND ESTABLISH PRIORITIES

Identify specific, realistic but challenging goals for yourself so that your time management has some purpose. Don't let perfectionist standards waste your time, if the task doesn't require them. Establishing priorities makes sure that you spend time on the things that really matter to you (e.g. your loved ones).

2   SPOT THE TIME WASTERS

Later in the chapter you will be shown 50 ways to stop wasting your time. But, first of all, think about how you spend your time. This might give you some clues about how to save it: speaking (both in public and private), travelling, sleeping, leisure, shopping, writing, conflict resolution, waiting, eating and drinking.

3   LIVE TIME MANAGEMENT

Be ruthlessly self-disciplined and always time conscious. Use every minute of the day to achieve your personal goals – take care of the minutes and the hours will look after themselves. Remember the *value* of your time – time past is gone for ever.

4   THINK QUALITY NOT QUANTITY OF TIME

Time management is about using your time better, not necessarily working harder. You must use as little time as possible to achieve your work goals so that you can give more time to your leisure and loved ones. Don't believe that it's smart to work long hours for the sake of it. So organise yourself.

5   ORGANISE YOURSELF FOR SUCCESS

Here are some tips to use your time better:

● *Act purposefully and positively*   Begin each activity

with a clear understanding of what you want to achieve and then think positively about doing it. Remember that your boss can help or hinder your time management.

- *Be proactive*   Take the initiative, anticipate events and take responsibility for your personal attitudes and actions.
- *Seek and benefit from the help of others, where necessary*   If you can, have a secretary to deal with your clerical chores and to help you with your time management.
- *Stay healthy in body and mind*   This is important, to enable you to think clearly of ways to improve your organisation. Control stress and get enough sleep.
- *Battle with paper*   Don't drown in piles of paper. If in doubt, throw it out. Only keep something which you *use on a regular basis*. Throw away junk mail as soon as you receive it.
- *Improve your filing and storage*   Store things near where you need them. Have to hand items that you use on a regular basis, such as keys, scissors, pens. Use filing cabinets with hanging folders for easy reference.
- *Clear your desk*   Start and end each day with a tidy desk. This raises the morale and helps to clear your mind. Only things related to one task should be on the desk at any one time. Richard Branson is a firm believer in working at an empty desk with only a pen and a piece of paper. But don't do what they did at Marks and Spencer after a 'clear your desk' campaign: people just transferred the piles of paper to underneath their desks. So they couldn't even sit down!
- *Look at your bookshelves*   Only keep reference books and those books you use regularly or want for sentimental reasons. Give the books you're never going to read to a charity shop.
- *Avoid interruptions*   In particular, get away from the telephone as much as you can. Screen your calls with an answerphone. Quality time is uninterrupted time, so try to work when nobody else is around (e.g. early morning) and work at home as much as possible. If you think an appointment will go on a long time, arrange another

appointment after, say, an hour. This will give you an excuse to end the conversation amiably. Use body language to signify that a conversation is over – lean forward in your seat as if to get up, and start gathering together your papers. Alternatively stand and start moving towards the door.

- **Don't get bogged down in detail** Think clearly and concentrate on the important matters. Delegate everything else, if you can.
- **Look before you leap** Calmly work out the best way of doing something before you start.
- **Prioritise** Give your undivided attention to doing the important things really well.
- **Don't believe anyone who says 'It will only take a minute'** Nothing takes only a minute. Don't deal with the matter immediately, but fix a time to give it the attention it deserves.

6 WRITE A DAILY TIME LOG

Complete a table with the following columns for each day:

1 **Time** In half hour intervals from the time you get up to the time you go to bed.
2 **Activity** What you do in each half hour.
3 **Priority** Mark each activity according to how important it is (A: extremely important; B: important; C: relatively unimportant).
4 **Effectiveness** In this column take note of how effectively each activity helped you to achieve your goals, and the reasons why you failed or succeeded.

Then at the end of each day evaluate it. Ask yourself:

- Have I been using my time to achieve my goals effectively?
- Have I got enough uninterrupted time?
- Have I been devoting enough time to the really important things?

If not, do something about it!

7 WORK TO SUIT YOUR PREFERRED LIFESTYLE

Make sure that your work satisfies your individual needs as far as possible. It must fit into the way you want to lead your life. So mould your job to your requirements and don't accept that it must be boring and soul destroying. To do this:

- *Actively seek challenges in your work* Invent them, if necessary. Work is what you make of it.
- *Stay optimistic and think positive* Great expectations breed success. Look upon your work as an opportunity for personal growth and achievement and do four things at work:

  1 Avoid blaming yourself for your failures and give yourself credit for your successes.
  2 Realise that mistakes usually only have a temporary effect.
  3 Don't let mishaps or down days affect other areas of your life.
  4 Don't angrily accept obstacles and problems but find ways around them.

- *Build flexibility into your job* If you don't already, ask your boss if it would be possible to work at different times (maybe early in the mornings or later at night) to fit into your daily schedule. For example, you may want to pick up the children from school, or do some shopping in midweek when the shops are quieter. Some of you might have this flexitime already – such working practices have become increasingly popular in recent years. If you can't get such flexibility from your job, it might be worth moving to one that can. If not, working for yourself, perhaps at home, can give you greater flexibility.
- *Stand out from the crowd* Don't work late if your colleagues or boss are putting moral pressure on you to do so. Explain that your family and leisure are important to you, and they improve your work performance by making you a more purposeful, happier person. If you are

particularly busy and have a deadline to meet, ask to work at home, so that you have the flexibility to look after your family. Remember you have the right to be happy in your life.

- *Leave a job if your employer won't make it attractive for you* It's only a job after all. Remember it's *your* life and the people who really count are your loved ones. So put them first.

50 Ways To Save Time

1 Remember the golden rule of time management: **It's not how much time you spend but how well you use it.**
2 *Improve effectiveness of meetings through:*

- Preparing yourself and others – use clear and concise agendas.
- Choosing a strong chairperson.
- Setting time guidelines for action.
- Agreeing the duration and sticking to it. Holding a meeting near the end of the day is a great incentive to finish on time!
- Avoiding unnecessary meetings.
- Avoiding inviting people who waffle, and make clear to everyone who does attend they should be concise and to the point.
- Avoiding interruptions.
- Holding meetings in rooms without any chairs. Meetings generally take less time if people can't sit down!
- Holding the meetings in other people's offices – it's easier to leave!

3 *Only speak in public if it achieves your own personal goals. Keep social chit-chat to a minimum.*
4 *Read faster and improve your memory* (see pages 31 to 34)

5 *The length of time talking to someone should be solely dependent upon the importance of the conversation* Remember standing discussions take much less time than sitting ones. So stand up if the office chatterbox arrives! Practise and use conversation-stopping phrases like: 'Well then, we have agreed to do ...' 'What you said is interesting. I'll consider it and come back to you.' Use coffee breaks or lunch times for short discussions.

6 *Learn to say no* Be assertive, and defend your right not to have your time wasted.

7 *Say what you mean in the shortest possible time.*

8 *Find the minimum amount of sleep you need and stick to it* Remember too much sleep can be counter-productive.

9 *Keep travelling time to a minimum* Set off and come home early to avoid traffic. Work at home as much as you can. Move house to reduce commuting time. Listen to the traffic news on the radio to avoid traffic jams.

10 *Use travelling time* Listen to a book tape in the car, do a correspondence course or just relax listening to some music. Travel by train and do something constructive during the journey.

11 *Concentrate, and check things only once* Don't waste time double checking.

12 *Don't check people's work unnecessarily* Delegate effectively.

13 *Don't forget or misplace things* Put things in their proper place. Also write check lists, shopping lists, and 'to do' lists (mark tasks urgent, 'some time today', or 'could wait'). Start each day with such a list which tells you what you need to do that day.

14 *Methodically go up and down each aisle at the supermarket* Don't zig-zag, and avoid going back for things at the other end of the shop. Write your shopping list according to where the goods are in the store. Try to shop on quiet days – Mondays and Tuesdays, avoiding Thursdays, Fridays and Saturdays if you can.

15 *Use waiting time* Think, read, write. Always carry

something to read and a little book to write good ideas or thoughts in. Minimise waiting time by taking the first appointment of the day.

16 *Write concisely and avoid unnecessary communication* Don't dictate replies to memos. Telephone or write a brief reply on a photocopy of the memo.

17 *Use a calendar* Make sure your appointments don't clash. Every Sunday spend ten minutes looking at the calendar for the week ahead and completing a 'to do' list (see Point 13).

18 *Try to do two things at the same time* Combine ironing and watching TV, and always take something up/downstairs with you.

19 *Don't be a slave to the TV* Select what you want – don't let yourself watch rubbish!

20 *Think ahead and anticipate problems* Prepare things the night before (e.g. packed lunches).

21 *Be time conscious but don't clock-watch* Be fanatical about not wasting time. Value your time.

22 *Use technological aids but don't play with them!* Computers, answering machines, dictaphones, electronic mail, fax, mobile telephones, electrical household appliances (microwave, dishwasher, food processor etc) all have their place. A dishwasher saves the average family about 25 minutes a day!

23 *Prepare meals in bulk and freeze them* Plan meals in advance.

24 *Avoid interruptions and get away from the telephone as much as you can* Employ a secretary, if you can, to take important calls. Use an answering machine or take the phone off the hook.

25 *Remember it is legitimate to be unavailable some of the time.*

26 *Get organised* See the fifth principle of time management on pages 53 to 55.

27 *Don't procrastinate* Be decisive. Nip potentially explosive situations in the bud before they become a time consuming headache.

28 *Make sure you have all the information you need to make a decision promptly and effectively.*

29 **Do things right first time**   Improve your work effectiveness by working when you are at your best – early in the morning or late at night.

30 **Listen effectively**   (see page 97).

31 **Tackle most unpleasant tasks first**   This will cut down on worry time.

32 **Eat sandwiches during the day for flexibility and speed**   Eat healthy fast food for energy, though. Use your lunch hour once a week for a specific activity.

33 **Keep your mind and body in shape**   This will give you the energy and peace of mind to deal speedily and effectively with life's problems. Have a tough mind to keep busy when the going gets rough. Relax, because relaxation clears your mind to think better. Remember illness wastes time.

34 **Stay cool**   Panic clouds the mind and wastes time. Keep your sense of humour to see you through a crisis. Don't waste your time worrying – just get on with life!

35 **Remember that time is money.**

36 **Seize the day!**   Grab your opportunities and make the most of the present.

37 **Don't let your punctuality penalise you**   If people are regularly late for meetings, you do the same.

38 **Have purpose in your life**   This gives you the motivation to use your time well.

39 **Set yourself specific, realistic and challenging goals**   Every task should have a deadline for completion.

40 **Prioritise**   Concentrate on what's important.

41 **Use a mental or written time log**   (see the sixth principle of time management on page 55).

42 **Have work flexibility if you can**   (see the seventh principle on page 56).

43 **Get out of bed as soon as you wake up.**

44 **Take a shower not a bath.**

45 **Pay people to do jobs around the house if you can.**

46 **Delegate**   Ask yourself: 'Do I have to do this or can I ask somebody else to do it?' Trust other people to do things for you! Don't over-supervise! A good way to remember this is the '4D rule' suggested by the *BBC*

time management book, *Making Time,* by G. Hargreaves, D. Morfett and G. Bown:

> Drop it
> Delay it
> Delegate it
> or, if all else fails, Do it!

47 *Remember Parkinson's Law: Work expands to fill the time available.*
48 *Keep your time spent on routine chores to a minimum.*
49 *Educate other people in time management* Then they won't waste your time.
50 *Simplify your grooming, cut down your wardrobe to the essentials and decide the night before what you are going to wear the next day.*

One Final Reminder

Remember the golden rule of time management: 'It's not how much time you spend but how well you use it.' Life is too short to waste time. As Benjamin Franklin wrote, 'Do not squander time, for that's the stuff life is made of.'

7

STAY HEALTHY AND ENERGETIC

This chapter will show you how to:

▶ *Keep physically fit*

▶ *Eat well but stay healthy*

▶ *Have the energy for the things you've always wanted to do*

YOU ARE GIVEN only one body, so make the best of it. Fitness helps to make you happy, gives you the energy to do things, and releases endorphins – the body's natural painkillers – which help to calm your nerves. Poorer health means a shorter life to enjoy. This chapter is, therefore, particularly important in making the most of your potential. It discusses seven principles for healthy living, but first let's assess how healthy you are now.

How Healthy Are You?

1 Do you take positive steps to improve your health?
2 Do you make a conscious effort to eat low fat foods?
3 Do you think you deal well with stress?
4 Do you take exercise every day?

5 Do you get enough sleep?

6 Do you have the energy to do the things you want to do?

7 Do you have a positive attitude to life?

8 Do you believe in the possibility of illness?

9 Do you believe you have some control over your own health?

10 Do you recognise self-destructive habits when you see them?

The more 'yes' answers you have, the healthier your lifestyle. But even if you said 'yes' to every one, there is always room for improvement. All of you should read carefully the following principles of good health.

Principles of Healthy Living

HEALTH PRINCIPLE NO 1: WATCH YOUR DIET

In both Britain and America there is an obsession with dieting and slimming. Americans alone spend over $30 billion per year on diets and related services. One of the most famous dieters today is chat show superstar Oprah Winfrey. In 1988 she was wearing size 10 jeans, but by the middle of 1992 she had put all the weight back on – like 95 per cent of all dieters, according to research. Where did she go wrong? She binged after the diet. Now Oprah is slim again and successfully keeping her weight down. She does this by exercising vigorously twice a day, being mentally tough, and eating low fat foods. Diet is as important to your looks as it is to your health. It is also vital for children. Research in Britain shows that a poor diet in early life can adversely affect the chances of academic success and getting a good job. So here are some points of information about a healthy diet:

● *Eat lots of fruit and vegetables* They're full of

vitamins, minerals and fibre. Every day consume two servings of fruit (either a medium piece of fresh fruit or five ounces of juice) and three servings of vegetables. An apple a day really does keep the doctor away – the Imperial Cancer Research Fund believes that people who eat one piece of fruit a day have a 30 to 50 per cent lower risk of stomach cancer. These vegetables can also help protect you against cancer: carrots, sweet potatoes, spinach, tomatoes, turnips, broccoli, cabbage, brussels sprouts, cauliflower, and radishes.

- *Get your protein the healthy way* Choose lean cuts of fish, meat and poultry. Grill or bake rather than fry them. Red meat is higher in fat, so eat fish or poultry at least two or three times a week. Wholemeal bread, rice, baked beans and jacket potatoes are also filling, low on calories (it's what you have with them that makes them fattening) and also excellent sources of fibre and protein.
- *Don't be too hard on dairy products* They give you valuable vitamins, minerals and protein. Milk also helps to get you off to sleep, but doesn't help ulcers unfortunately. Go for the low fat alternatives and remember that eggs are relatively high in cholesterol, which causes heart disease. Recent research shows that butter may not be as bad for you as you think, however. It seems that butter is no worse for you than full fat margarine. It's how much you put on that counts!
- *Go steady on oil and fatty foods* Watch your intake of chips, cakes, biscuits, flans, pies and sausages. Reduce your intake of saturated fats and cholesterol, particularly present in animal fats. Don't overdo it though – you need a certain amount of cholesterol for a healthy diet. Just enjoy fat, but be sensible and don't go mad. Remember that fatty foods increase your risk of cancer, and you also increase your chances of diabetes, high blood pressure and heart disease if you are overweight. But olive oil (particularly virgin oil) and oily fish (such as tuna and mackerel) have been proved to be good for your heart.
- *Reduce your salt intake* Salt raises your blood pressure, which can lead to heart problems. On average we eat 12 times more salt than we need.

- **Cut down on sugar** Sugar is present not only in the obvious things like chocolate but also in some processed foods like pies. Sugar is not only high in calories, of course, but also reduces your energy levels after temporarily increasing them (see the fourth principle of healthy living on page 70)
- **Enjoy yourself** Your diet shouldn't make you miserable, so treat yourself occasionally. But eat sensibly and acknowledge the benefits of a healthy diet. Healthy foods are not necessarily unexciting – in fact, they can be really tasty, so try them!
- **Remember the children** Under-fives need plenty of calories and lots of high calorie, high fat food. There is evidence that giving children only low fat foods can cause possible brain damage and undernourishment. So don't off-load your healthy eating habits on to your children.
- **Vitamin pills are no substitute for a good diet** The complexity of the interactions between the various components in foods cannot be copied artificially. Don't take iron supplements unless recommended by your doctor. In 1992 a study of 1,900 Finnish men found that high iron levels were second only to smoking in increasing the risk of a heart attack. But if for some reason you aren't getting a good, balanced diet, multi-vitamin pills will help you.
- **Fill yourself with fibre** Wholegrain cereals, fruit and vegetables help prevent bowel cancer and constipation. Remember laxatives are no long-term answer. Soluble fibre in oats and pulses helps lower blood cholesterol.
- **Drink lots of water** Two pints a day can prevent constipation and clear the skin.
- **Eat regularly** Stomach acids increase if you don't eat for long periods.
- **Remember going out for business lunches needn't be an unhealthy experience** Make sure you can do an afternoon's work afterwards!
- **Be obsessive about hygiene** Clean work surfaces and chopping boards. Have a separate board for raw meat – you'd be surprised how much salmonella a raw chicken has. Wash fruit and vegetables well. Cook everything thor-

oughly and according to the instructions on the packet. Make sure all meat from the freezer has completely defrosted.

- **Chew it** Chew food well and eat slowly. This helps your digestion system and reduces flatulence. Savour every bite and you'll find that you will need less of what you're eating.
- **Eat to live not live to eat** It was Benjamin Franklin who uttered these wise words. Eating should help you lead a better life, not enslave you.
- **Snack your way to health** Eat snacks of low fat food when you feel peckish – fruit, raw carrot, celery etc. No biscuits or chocolate! There is also some evidence that eating your diet in lots of mini meals rather than in three square meals can reduce harmful cholesterol.
- **Eat a good breakfast** Eating too little at breakfast is self-defeating. It won't be long before you start craving food later in the morning, when the only thing available may be an unhealthy snack. Eat a good healthy breakfast instead.
- **Don't ignore hunger** The important thing is to eat healthily when you are hungry.
- **Watch artificial sweeteners** There is some evidence that these may stimulate the appetite.
- **Foods can affect your moods** Mangoes and pomegranates can brighten you up, but too much cabbage, broccoli, swede, soya beans, or peas can mildly depress you. Lettuce, parsley, radishes and potatoes can relax you and even make you sleepy! Horseradish, fennel and spring onions do the reverse.
- **Enough is as good as a feast** Always stop eating while you're still a little hungry.
- **Think before you buy organic** There is little evidence that there is much nutritional advantage in organic food. However, it is chemical-free, although the medical profession don't know whether residues of fertiliser or pesticides do you any harm. Organic farming is also much kinder to the countryside.

HEALTH PRINCIPLE NO 2: WATCH THE BOOZE AND DON'T SMOKE!

One or even two (small) drinks a day can help your heart, but don't overdo it. The current government safe limits are 21 units a week for men and 14 units for women (a unit is a half pint of beer, a glass of wine, or a pub measure of spirits). These limits might be revised slightly upwards because of the positive effects of moderate drinking on heart disease, but there is no doubt that excessive drinking is positively harmful. It can cause cancer, hepatitis, cirrhosis of the liver, high blood pressure, depression, stomach disorders, sexual difficulties and brain damage. The government says that men start to increase the risk of such problems if they drink 36 units or more in a week, and for women it is 22 units. Excessive drinking in one evening can even kill you. During 1987 in England and Wales alone, 213 people died from alcohol poisoning.

Drinking also kills your brain cells, so too much boozing means much less quality thinking. Alcohol harms people other than the drinker – up to 50 per cent of murders involve alcohol, and three people die in Britain every day due to a drunken driver. One in three divorces are due to behavioural problems linked to drinking. It also does no good for the economy. In 1989 it cost British industry £1.7 billion through higher absenteeism and accident rates, bad decision making and lower productivity. Drinkers are three times more likely to have accidents than other workers, and take four times as many days off. The problem is widespread and getting worse. There are at least 300,000 people in the UK whose drinking problem is so bad that they are 'alcohol dependent', and 10 per cent of the workforce have problems with alcohol. Don't be one of them.

The hazards of smoking are well known – lung cancer and bronchitis. A recent study in America also found that smoking can reduce men's sexual potency. There is concern that the risk of brain cancer or leukaemia may be 30 per cent higher in children whose mothers smoked during pregnancy. Passive smoking also increases the chances of both lung cancer and heart disease. You don't have to be exposed to smoke for very long before it becomes harmful. One study found that rabbits developed lung damage after being exposed to passive smoke for 15 minutes a day for only 20 days. There is also evidence that lower tar cigarettes are 30 per cent more harmful to passive smokers than higher tar brands. Passive smoking is now causing concern for employers, particularly after the Veronica Bland case in Britain. In January 1993 Bland won a £15,000 out-of-court settlement after it was found that passive smoking at work had played an important part in her bronchitis. Today eight out of nine employers restrict smoking in some way, and an increasing number are banning it altogether.

What about the argument that smoking keeps your weight down? Smoking does slightly increase your metabolism, but the effect is so small that giving up would only increase your weight by an extra pound per month. All you have to do to overcome this weight gain is to reduce your calorie intake by 70 calories a day and take some brisk exercise (which also reduces the pain of giving up by generating endorphins, the body's natural painkillers). So don't just cut down your smoking or switch to low tar cigarettes. Stop it altogether before it's too late for you and those around you. Remember on average for each cigarette smoked you take about five and a half minutes off your life. Ex-Marlboro man, Wayne McClaren, said days before he died, 'Tobacco will kill you and I am dying proof of it.'

HEALTH PRINCIPLE NO 3: EXERCISE!

Regular exercise is good for you. It keeps you in shape, increases your energy levels, keeps your heart healthy and relieves stress. Exercise can also help headaches, back pain, insomnia, stiffness, painful joints and bowel irregularity. You don't necessarily have to jog or play a sport – brisk walking and putting more effort into everyday chores will do. Build walking into your routine and walk rather than using the car or lift. How often do you use the stairs at work? Pursue an energetic hobby like gardening, swimming, cycling or dancing. The important thing is to do what you enjoy – for example, give your walks some worthwhile purpose such as collecting the newspapers or going to the pub. You won't keep on exercising regularly if you don't think it's fun. This is the mistake that many people make when they jog or buy an exercise bike. Exercise becomes a chore, something they dread.

Exercise together with a low fat diet is the best, permanent way to lose weight and look good. After strenuous exercise you also get what is sometimes called 'after burn' – exercise boosts your metabolism so you use up calories even after you've finished exercising. But don't make exercise too strenuous – excess fat is removed by slow, moderate exercise. You can tell whether you're exercising at this rate by speaking or singing out loud. If you're a little breathless, but can still be understood, you're OK. For weight loss and a healthy heart you should be doing such exercise three to five times a week for at least 15–20 minutes. As you get fitter you can increase this to 30–45 minutes. Always consult your doctor before starting any exercise programme, if you are over 40, have been ill or haven't exercised for some time. Obviously different forms of exercise burn up different amounts of calories in an hour, as follows:

Walking at 2mph	165	Jogging at 10mph	1350
Walking at 4mph	475	Rowing	1090
Cycling at 13mph	660	Golf	284
Tennis	428	Dancing	300
Jogging at 6mph	770	Gardening	280
Jogging at 8mph	1075	Brisk swimming	480

There is evidence that exercise improves your health at any age. In America 60- and 70-year-old men became as fit and energetic after an exercise programme as people 20 to 30 years younger. Research also shows that exercise improves your mood, gives you a more optimistic outlook on life, makes you more creative by increasing your clarity of thought and improves your sex life. Finally, remember the remark of a former American Surgeon General, that the health equivalent of not exercising is smoking a packet of cigarettes every day.

HEALTH PRINCIPLE NO 4: BOOST YOUR ENERGY

People like Margaret Thatcher only need four or five hours sleep, and they still have boundless energy. Are you like this, or do you struggle to find the energy to do all the things you want to do? If so, read these tips on how to become more energetic:

- *Eat well*   Cut down on fats as they make you drowsy. Witness what you feel like after the Sunday roast or a big plate of fish and chips! Reduce your intake of high sugar foods like chocolate. Sugar supplies a quick boost of energy, but then your body wants more sugar almost immediately. If you don't give it what it wants, your body rebels and you will feel tired. Something else to think about is replacing three big meals with smaller meals at shorter intervals. This may help you to keep your energy without resorting to unhealthy snacks or excessive caffeine. Avoid eating foods to which you are allergic, or which contain the amino acid tryptophan, except late in the evening. This makes you drowsy and sleepy. Foods high in tryptophan are:

Chicken	Liver	Parmesan cheese
Cottage cheese	Macaroni	Peanut butter
Eggs	Milk	Rice
Oatmeal	Nuts	Tuna
Ice cream		

Unless you want to go to sleep, reduce your intake of these foods. Finally, eat lots of vegetables and complex carbohydrates (e.g. pasta, rice, baked potatoes) and drink lots of water. Research shows that they can make you more energetic. Water removes waste from your system without flushing out essential vitamins and minerals, as coffee or soft drinks can.

- *Cut down on caffeine and alcohol*   Use decaffeinated coffee or tea and drink non-alcoholic drinks as much as you can. Alcohol and caffeine can rob your body of important nutrients, and also cause excessive highs and lows which reduce your energy and make you sleepy. Caffeine may give you a temporary energy boost but, as with sugar, soon afterwards your body craves for more, and you feel more tired if it doesn't get it.

- **Exercise** Slumping in front of the TV won't do too much for your energy. It's exercise which gives you stamina (see health principle three on page 68). Yoga breathing and stretching exercises also boost your mental and physical energy. Stomach crunches can help, too. Lie on your back with knees bent and then lift your shoulders a couple of inches from the floor.

- **Breathe effectively** You should breathe from the stomach rather than the chest. If you breathe from your chest, your breathing is too quick and shallow and so ultimately more tiring.

- **Control stress** Stress can be an important cause of constant tiredness.

- **Get a good night's sleep** Avoid within two hours of bedtime: caffeine in tea, coffee and chocolate, smoking and alcohol (all three speed up your heart beat); strenuous exercise (except sex, which is good for sleep), and eating a large meal. Consume things with tryptophan in them, warm milk is particularly good for sleep. Remember not to worry about lack of sleep. Worrying about insomnia usually causes far more damage than sleeplessness. Other things you can do to help you sleep are:

  a **Control stress** Do some relaxation exercises just before bedtime, and get as much exercise as possible during the day.

  b **Conquer your fears and anxieties.** (See page 16.)

  c **Find peace of mind** Remember to keep your problems in perspective – they are probably not as important as you think. Don't take your worries to bed with you. Talk them through with somebody, and forget about them before your head hits the pillow.

  d **Don't oversleep** Too much sleep is just as damaging for energy as too little. Find the amount of sleep that's right for you and stick to it. Researchers say the average optimum requirement is 7½ to 8 hours, but many people survive perfectly well on less. Research shows that the average person can reduce his or her sleep permanently to six hours without impairing performance. Reduce your sleep slowly by taking 15 minutes off it every night. Bear in mind that a 20-minute nap in the early afternoon can help you survive on less sleep at night.

e *Stop taking sleeping pills* Don't become dependent on them, because they are not a long-term answer.

f *Establish a regular sleep routine* Follow the same rituals every night, e.g. filling the hot water bottle, making a milky drink etc. Always try to be in bed by a certain time. There is something in the old saying that an hour's sleep before midnight is worth two after it.

g *Act positively if you waken in the night* Relax in bed for a while and let sleep return. Try reading, listening to music, or relaxation exercises. If these don't work, do something and then return to bed when you're sleepy.

● *Try alternative medicine* Aromatherapy, acupuncture (called acupressure if needles aren't used), reflexology, the Alexander technique, yoga, homeopathy, shiatsu massage and tai chi (meditative movement) can all release energy. Contact your local library for more information about them.

● *Don't be a perfectionist if it isn't necessary* Perfectionism can burn up your energy.

● *Take shorter holidays* Several short holidays boost your energy better than one long holiday.

● *Be happy and positive* Optimism and loving life are great sources of energy. Have passion, fun and excitement in your life through the right balance between your work and leisure. Psychologists say that workaholics often burn out in mid-career. People with balance are more likely to have the stamina to last. Author Ann McGhee-Cooper suggests that we should recapture the vitality of childhood by spontaneously jumping from one interest to another; smiling and laughing more; experiencing and expressing emotions freely; being physically active; dreaming and imagining; and believing in the impossible. Go for it!

- **Be self-motivated** Let your willpower overcome fatigue. Give yourself purpose and be self-disciplined. Self-motivation can also come from surviving deep, personal crises. One leading American executive had to care for his wife, who was dying of cancer, as well as his two children. Now he views any problem as easy by comparison.

- **Remember fatigue shouldn't be a status symbol** Just because everyone else at work is tired and working long hours doesn't mean that you have to make the same mistakes. Use your time better to do more in a shorter time.

- **Check yourself for Seasonal Affective Disorder (SAD)** This is a form of depression which tires you. It normally happens in the winter because it's caused by lack of sunlight. It can be easily treated with light therapy, so ask your doctor.

- **Observe what drains your energy** Do something about it before you are completely exhausted.

- **Don't dwell on worry and guilt** It's exhausting! Try to let go of your stored up anger and grief.

HEALTH PRINCIPLE NO 5: KNOW YOUR AILMENTS

To stay healthy you should have some basic information about ailments which you might have, or be apprehensive about. The important ones are as follows:

CANCER

Cancer is the second commonest cause of death in Britain after heart disease. The things you can do to avoid the disease according to author Dr Barry Lynch in his book *The BBC Health Check* are:

- Stop smoking.
- Go easy on alcohol.

- Avoid being overweight.
- Cut down on fatty foods.
- Eat more fibre, fruit and vegetables.
- Don't expose yourself too much to the sun – this can cause skin cancer.
- Observe the health and safety regulations at work.
- See your doctor if you have the following symptoms:

  a a lump anywhere in the body
  b a sore that doesn't heal
  c a skin mole which is increasing in size
  d any unusual bleeding e.g. in your water or bowel motions
  e any bleeding from the vagina or front passage after the menopause
  f any mucus or discharge from the back passage
  g a change in bowel habits (like constipation, diarrhoea or the two alternating)
  h a persistent cough or hoarseness
  i any unexplained weight loss

- Have a regular cervical smear test.
- Examine your breasts every month – look out for any lumps or anything unusual.
- Check your testicles for cancer, preferably every month. Do this after a shower or bath when the scrotal skin is relaxed. If one testicle feels heavier than the other or one of the testicles feels unusual, you should consult your doctor.
- Watch out for cancer of the prostate, which is three times more common in men than cervical cancer in women. Try to have regular checkups.

If you find out that you have cancer, try not to panic. Many types of cancer are curable, particularly if you catch them early. So be vigilant and remember that your spirit – the will to live – can be a potent weapon in the fight against the disease.

HEART DISEASE
Heart attacks are the main cause of death in Britain, but again there are certain things we can do to try and avoid them:

- Stop smoking and reduce excess drinking (see health principle two on page 67).
- Cut down on saturated fats to reduce cholesterol and eat lots of fibre, e.g. in fruit and vegetables.
- Do something about high blood pressure. To do this follow all the tips to prevent heart disease and reduce your salt intake. Doctors recommend that everyone between the ages of 20 and 65 should have their blood pressure checked at least once every five years.
- Lose weight if you have to.
- Exercise regularly.
- Reduce stress.

Finally, what are the warning signs of a heart attack? According to the British Heart Foundation they are:

a Uncomfortable pressure, squeezing or pain in the centre of the chest for at least 20 minutes.

b Pain spreading from the chest down into the arms (especially the left arm) and into the lower jaw or back.

c Sweating or pallor, breathlessness and fatigue, sometimes accompanied by fainting, nausea, or vomiting.

If in any doubt, call for an ambulance.

AIDS (ACQUIRED IMMUNE DEFICIENCY SYNDROME)

AIDS is the late stage of an infection, caused by HIV, or human immuno-deficiency virus. HIV is transmitted through sexual intercourse, blood transfusions, and sharing hypodermic needles. It can also be passed on from mother to child. A woman infected with HIV can pass the virus to her baby during pregnancy, during birth, or shortly after birth. It is *not* spread through casual contact – kissing, handshakes, eating from the same dish or drinking from the same glass. You also can't be infected at swimming pools, restaurants, or toilets.

DEPRESSION

Depression can affect us all. For example, it led to the suicide of the writer Ernest Hemingway. One in four women and one in seven men will suffer a serious bout of depression by the time they are 65. So what are the tell-tale signs? The main indicator is a sense of isolation. You feel utterly alone in an unescapable prison, that you can't carry on. You are absent from work more, you may drink and sleep more, but still feel tired. You also become more prone to illness, and depression has been found to precede serious diseases like cancer and heart failure.

A major cause of depression is the loss of self-confidence, which makes it impossible for the depressed person to make decisions – so re-read Chapter Two! Because of their stressful lifestyle, successful executives are particularly prone to depression. Depressed people need to re-discover their purpose in life and view any achievements positively. In addition they should use anti-depressant drugs (as a short-term measure) and seek help from a counsellor or psychotherapist to talk through their problems. Depression won't go away until the problems have been sorted out.

MENOPAUSE

The menopause is caused by a decline in hormones (particularly oestrogen, at the end of menstruation) and for some women it can cause adverse physical and psychological symptoms such as aches and pains, irritability, hot flushes and night sweats. Women in Britain reach menopause on average from the ages of 49 to 53. Hormone replacement therapy (HRT) is used as a successful treatment, but is not suitable for everyone. But remember the menopause doesn't mean the end of an enjoyable sex life!

BACKACHE

Back trouble is a big problem for many people, especially as they get older. To prevent problems, lift things with a straight back, and do pelvic thrust exercises to strengthen the muscles at the bottom of your spine. Ask your doctor for details. Much back trouble is also caused by sitting for long periods at a VDU and working at your desk, so make sure your desk and chair are at the right height, and you are the right distance from the screen.

HEALTH PRINCIPLE NO 6: DEAL EFFECTIVELY WITH YOUR DOCTOR

First of all, you need to choose the right doctor for you and your family. Try to go on personal recommendation, if you can. Then familiarise yourself with your rights when dealing with your doctor. You are entitled to:

- see your medical notes and those of children too young to make their own decisions, although your doctor can withhold information if he or she thinks it may damage your health.
- have someone with you during a consultation.
- confidentiality – your doctor can only discuss your case with other health workers.
- a second opinion (eg. from a consultant).

Before you go to the surgery make a note of your concerns and any questions you may have. Once you are in the surgery, state clearly what your symptoms are. Be assertive and don't be fobbed off, if you think that something is wrong. Knowledge is power, so keep informed about general health matters, but beware of becoming an amateur GP. Remember your doctor is the expert, so trust is important. Listen carefully to what you are told, and accept bad news as courageously as you can. Feel free to ask for as thorough an explanation as you want to have, making sure that you understand the answer. Try not to call your doctor late at night, or early on a Sunday morning, unless there is an emergency.

HEALTH PRINCIPLE NO 7: SPIRIT, THE WILL TO BE HEALTHY

Your attitude to life has a big impact on your health. For example, how you react to stressful events like bereavements and finding out you have a serious disease. You must have the will to live and something or somebody to live for. Then you will have the resolve and the inner strength to be healthy – think about your goals and the quality of your life. Try to avoid 'Type A' behaviour – hurried, aggressive, impatient and easily angered. People with Type A personalities are more likely to suffer from stress and heart diseases. Convert yourself to a more contemplative, relaxed 'Type B' personality. Slow down and ease up as much as you can. Reduce any mistrust you have of other people's motives, and learn to treat others with kindness and consideration. Forgive and forget.

Don't be too obsessed with having material possessions or looking good. British comedienne and actress Dawn French has said, 'I decided when I was six that I'd be big and happy as opposed to dieting and unhappy.' Avoid boredom by living your life for the people you love. Evidence shows that helping others will give you an emotional high. In return people will give you support when you really need it.

Most of all, think positively. Remember all the benefits you will get from a healthier lifestyle. Be proactive – *do something now* to make your life healthier. Don't wait until you are flat on your back in a hospital bed. Value your body – it is the only one you've got!

One Final Thought

'The first wealth is health', wrote American philosopher Ralph Waldo Emerson. There is nothing more precious than life itself. So treasure it.

8

BEAT STRESS AND FIND PEACE OF MIND

This chapter will show you how to:
- ▶ *Control stress in your life*
- ▶ *Find peace of mind*

STRESS is a well used word these days. Doctors and others blame it for a multitude of things. Famous people like the film star Judy Garland have suffered from it and turned to drugs and alcohol because of it. But what does the word stress mean to you? You might view it positively in terms of the challenge to do something really well. It would be accurate to call this pressure, which is very satisfying and makes your life worthwhile. Beware of the negative reactions to life's problems, however – anxiety, depression, a feeling that you have lost control over your life. This is what we shall call stress. Here are the top ten stress creators from researchers at the University of Washington (on a scale of 1 to 100 according to the amount of stress they produce):

Death of partner	100
Divorce	73
Separation	65
Jail sentence	63
Death of close family member	63
Serious injury or illness	53
Marriage	50

Being made redundant	47
Marital reconciliation	45
Retirement	45

Research also shows that stress hits women harder than men. This isn't terribly surprising when one remembers that many women have jobs and are still expected to do all the housework and look after the children. Stress is an increasing problem, too. It can give you sleeplessness, addictions (to alcohol, smoking, eating, and pills) headaches, stomach upsets, tension and irritability, impaired thinking, poor relations with other people, lower self-esteem, high blood pressure and ultimately heart problems. It can also make you less able to fight disease – 80 per cent of illnesses have been found to have a stress component in their development. Most of all, stress breaks your will to carry on, just like an increasing number of husbands and fathers who leave their home behind and disappear because they can't cope with financial, work and family worries.

In the USA employees with stress cost their employers on average $15,000 in medical treatment and time lost, and up to 15 per cent of American managers suffer from stress. In Britain stress-related illnesses account for 500 million working days lost every year. So what can be done about it. How can you control stress in your life? Here are some stress-beaters to help you.

Ten Stress-beaters

1 CHECK YOUR STAGE IN THE BURNOUT SCALE

Burnout is a term sometimes given to the degree to which stress is affecting your life. There are four stages in burnout – where are you?

a Energetic but increasingly uncertain Energy,

enthusiasm, overwork, uncertainty, doubts about coping, cancelling holidays, frustration with results.

b **First signs of anxiety** Short-lived bouts of irritation, tiredness and anxiety, feelings of stagnation, blaming others, unable to cope with work pressures, working long hours, ineffective time management.

c **General discontent** Anger, resentment, low self-esteem, guilt, apathy.

d **Withdrawal** Isolation, illness, absenteeism, alcohol and drug abuse.

2 BALANCE BETWEEN YOUR WORK AND LEISURE

At the end of the 1980s a survey of over 4,000 men in America indicated that 48 per cent of them felt their lives were empty and meaningless despite years of trying to attain professional success. Sixty-eight per cent felt they had neglected their families in their quest for success. John and Norma Major only spend the weekends together, because she's at home in Huntingdonshire and he's in London. So ask yourself the question: are you a workaholic? Find out by answering the following questions:

1 Do you wake up thinking about work?
2 Do you usually get up early, no matter how late you go to bed?
3 Have you given up leisure time for your work?
4 Do your family and friends think that you work too hard?
5 Are you usually the first to arrive at the office?
6 Do you sometimes work and eat at the same time?
7 Do you usually work in the evenings and weekends?
8 Do you find holidays a waste of time?
9 Do you dread retirement?
10 Do you really enjoy your work?

If you are answering 'yes' to all these questions you really are a workaholic. But does it matter? No, if you don't care about your relationships with other people. But of course most people do, and so finding a better balance between your work and leisure is essential. This isn't easy, particularly if you have young children. You must make time for your leisure, if you are going to lead a stress-free, happier and more worthwhile life. Pop star Sting has said: 'I think there's probably no better thing to have achieved at the end of your life than to have had a family that people are pleased to belong to.' If you have children, or would like them sometime, ask yourself: 'What is more important? Time at work, or time helping to raise a responsible human being?'

Be willing to work hard but within strict limits. Clearly define the boundaries between your work and leisure, and remember work isn't everything. It's your loved ones who must come first – don't forget that time spent at work is time not spent with them. Sir John Harvey-Jones, the extremely successful former boss of ICI, always kept his weekends work-free and gave up his naval career to spend more time with his daughter, who had polio.

Plan time for your life outside work – for holidays, leisure activities and relaxation. This will also help your work by re-charging your mental batteries. Research work by Paul Evans and Fernando Bartolomé in the USA shows that a better work/family balance actually increases managers' productivity. So re-evaluate your priorities in life. This is why in Britain 40 per cent of chief executives under the age of 50 are actively considering leaving their jobs, according to a research study by Professor Cary Cooper and Valerie Sutherland. They are fed up with a stressful, work-dominated life, with its adverse effects on their health, happiness and families. Always bear in mind the impact you have on others. Another research study has shown that children of divorced parents suffer psychological ill effects well into advanced life. Break free to beat stress! This is a subject we shall turn to in more detail in Chapter Thirteen.

3 RELAX!

Take time to relax – rest and reflection are crucial to productivity. Winston Churchill took one long nap almost every day, even during the Second World War. Learn to relax through the following tips:

- *Relaxation exercises* Slow deep breathing is a quick effective technique to relax during times of tension. Breathe in deeply, counting ten slowly, and then exhale doing the same thing. Do this for about 15 minutes. It really works. Another effective relaxation technique comes from yoga – tense your muscles whilst breathing in and then relax them when exhaling. Think about your muscles as you are doing it. Try this on your neck muscles in particular, because these often tense up when you are stressed.
- *Accept the past.*
- *Take regular exercise.*
- *Keep travelling to a minimum* Evidence shows it's tiring and stressful.
- *Make time for leisure* Have some fun!
- *Be creative* Creativity generates endorphins, which are your body's natural relaxers.
- *Reflection and meditation* Whatever method you use – prayer, transcendental meditation, yoga, tai chi – give yourself time on your own to reflect on your life.
- *Learn to pace yourself* Realise that you don't have to solve every problem you face overnight.
- *Go on relaxation courses* Contact your local library for information.
- *Don't kid yourself that smoking relaxes you* It does the reverse by speeding up your heartbeat. The only thing which relaxes you is the deep breathing.
- *Take short holidays* Shorter holidays are better for relieving stress than longer ones of the same total length, eg. take two separate weeks rather than one two-week holiday, if you can.
- *Don't rely on pills and tranquillisers as a permanent solution to stress* Don't become dependent on them.
- *Visualisation – or daydreaming!* Imagine yourself in a pleasurable, relaxing experience, e.g. lying on the beach in the sun.
- *Hypnosis* You might try this. It is not as cranky as it sounds and is now a widely accepted technique. Ask your GP to recommend a hypnotherapist. The professional

association of qualified hypnotherapists is the British Society of Medical and Dental Hypnosis.

- **Laugh** Keep your sense of humour.
- **Massage** This is very effective at calming you down.
- **Listen to music or play a musical instrument** Both can be very soothing.
- **Take a hot bath** Not too hot – around body temperature is best.
- **Have a good cry** Don't be afraid to, it's a great reliever of tension.
- **Let your mind go blank** Get rid of unwanted thoughts by just shutting your eyes and listening to every little sound around you.
- **Get some sleep** Don't accept disturbed sleep as inevitable when you're under pressure.
- **Do something about the causes of stress from the physical environment** Noise and poor light and ventilation all cause stress.
- **Childcare provision** Make sure you have good childcare arrangements, so that you are not worrying about your children when you are at work.

4 TALK ABOUT YOUR PROBLEMS

A problem shared is a problem halved. Talking a problem through with someone can put it into perspective and make it seem less insurmountable. If someone is annoying you, talk it through with them rather than bottling it up inside. Remain as cool and detached as you can. Close friends or relatives can also be a big help in times of stress. We all need a shoulder to cry on sometimes. You might also consider talking with someone else, like your priest or local GP.

5 COMMUNICATE ASSERTIVENESS

Improve your communication skills and learn to say no! See Chapters Three and Nine for more details on this.

6 IMPROVE YOUR TIME MANAGEMENT

Try to avoid doing too many stressful things at once. Live for the moment, but also plan time for yourself. Remember that a common cause of stress is too much work and too little time to do it. So reduce your workload if you can (e.g. through delegation and telling your boss you've got too much to do) and make the best possible use of your time (see Chapter 6 for more on this).

7 TALK TO YOURSELF

Give yourself encouragement by saying to yourself things like 'You can do it'; 'Your mind is calm'; 'You are in control'; 'What's the worst that could happen?' Often things are not as bad as they seem.

8 LOOK AFTER YOUR BODY

Watch out for early warning signs of stress – lack of concentration, irritability, perpetual tiredness, breathlessness, pumping heart, sweating, muscle aches and pains. Then do something immediately about the causes. Exercise, eat healthily, and don't smoke or drink too much alcohol, tea or coffee. Nicotine and large quantities of alcohol and caffeine actually make stress worse by speeding up your heartbeat.

9 STAY IN CONTROL

The international opera star Dame Kiri Te Kanawa has been successful and stress-free because she took control over her life when it mattered most. At the age of 22, she left a successful popular singing career at home in New Zealand to train as an opera singer in London. Her mother went with her, but Kiri began to resent her constant presence and interference. She had to do her own thing and asked her Mum to go back to New Zealand. There were many tears shed, but Kiri's new-found independence gave her the springboard to launch an incredibly successful and fulfilling career. You can do the same – reduce stress in your life by acting positively and assertively.

Concentrate on what you can do. Avoid negative or anxiety-provoking thoughts like: 'I can't cope'; 'What if ...?' Be proactive – try to anticipate changes in your life and do something about them before they hurt you. Keeping a stress diary will also enable you to cope better with the future. In it you should take note of any stressful events, what happened to your body and what you were thinking. This will help you to recognise stress more easily, to do something about it immediately, and avoid repeating the mistakes you previously made in reaction to it.

Stand by your rights when dealing with other people at home and at work, without losing your temper. Don't just explode when you are under stress. Take a deep breath, stand back and think about how you should react calmly to the situation.

Re-assess your job and its role in your life. Try to negotiate a certain amount of autonomy and flexibility in your job. Sort out any conflicts between your work as an employee with the other roles you have in your life – parent, husband/wife, partner, friend, son or daughter. Be clear and realistic about what you want to achieve in each of these roles and then go for it. If you are worried about losing your job, do something about it. Plan ahead, think what job you would like and start preparing for this – gaining necessary qualifications, talking to prospective employers, etc.

10 SEEK FUN WITH FULFILMENT

Enjoy yourself by doing something worthwhile and interesting, because boredom is a major cause of stress. Don't worry about tomorrow. Experience the joy of helping others. Find the right job, and have the courage to successfully cope with life's problems. Such strength will come from finding your inner peace and spiritual purpose in life – the final subject of this chapter.

How to Find Peace of Mind

Woody Allen is a comic genius. Lines like: 'My Brain? It's my second favourite organ' ring sweetly in the ears. But one can't escape the conclusion that he has found peace of mind elusive. He is a depressive neurotic who suffered psychologically from countless childhood moves and a tempestuous, unhappy relationship between his mother and father. Richard Burton also seemed to have everything. He was handsome and a great actor, with one of the finest voices of all time – a superstar. Yet Burton led a tormented life, which his one-time three bottles of vodka a day could not help him forget. He aimed to be a man he could be proud of, who would look after his family and friends, and his sadness was that he failed. In particular he felt guilty about leaving Jessica, the daughter of his first marriage. She was a beautiful schizophrenic, and her shadow always haunted him.

So what price peace? There are four things you can do to achieve peace of mind:

- **be true to the right values**
- **be at one with yourself**
- **accept the past, live for today and look to the future**
- **spiritual liberation.**

Let's look at each of these in a bit more detail.

PEACEMAKER NO 1: BE TRUE TO THE RIGHT VALUES

Dennis Levine, Wall Street insider dealer, was one of America's corporate heroes in the 1980s. In seven years he turned $39,750 into $11.5 million. He loved his work because he was doing a job he could do well. But Levine was breaking the law, and he paid the price – fury from his wife, shame in front of his family and jail. His arrest reduced his career to nothing. His ambition was so strong that he had forgotten about ethical behaviour. He knew that he was doing wrong, but told himself it was harmless. If only Levine had known that his baby daughter Sarah would learn to walk in a prison visiting room.

Levine's tragic story illustrates that you need the right values to influence the people who really matter. Don't make the same mistakes as he did. Be true to yourself and your values. Don't live a lie, but keep your integrity as a human being. Have the courage to be the person you want to be. Values give you not only courage but also a worthwhile purpose in life. They tell you what you ought to be and do, and so give you a clear conscience and tranquillity. Values help you to master your passions and desires. If you made love to everyone you fancied, you would not only be exhausted but also lose the peace that real love can bring! Research shows that a value system motivates you, builds your self-esteem, relieves stress, protects you from the hostility of others and wins friendship. Values also produce moral attitudes which create order and routine in your life, allowing you to make better use of opportunities and have the self-discipline and responsibility to achieve your goals.

But what values should you have? There are two questions to ask yourself here. What values influence your behaviour? What do you value in your life? Look at the two lists below. Rank them in order of importance, and work out what your priorities are. To do this ask yourself: Is a value right? Is it fair? Will I harm anyone by doing it? Would I tell my child to do it? Does it feel like the right thing to do? When answering these questions, it is worth remembering the philosophy of chat-show superstar Oprah Winfrey: 'Anything is valid if it helps people.'

VALUES INFLUENCING YOUR BEHAVIOUR

Impartiality

Honesty

Trustworthiness

Fairness, justice

Pursuit of excellence in everything you do

Compassion for others

Self-sacrifice – putting others first

Integrity

Humility

Loyalty

Faith – belief in something that is good and worth striving for

Hope – keeping alive a desire for good, and expectation of things to come

Prudence – taking the trouble to think out what you are doing, and what is likely to come of it

Temperance – moderation in all things, and self-discipline

Reliability

Courage – to do what you think is right

Courtesy

Patience

Keeping promises

WHAT YOU VALUE

Balance between work and personal life
Challenge
Autonomy
People contact
Creativity
Physical fitness
Peace of mind
Security
Helping others
Variety in what you do
Money
Power and status
Appearance
What other people think
Close friends
Close partner
Mixing with people
Being alone
Achieving your goals
Being the best in everything you do
Contributing to society
Happy family life
Happiness
Doing your own thing
Job satisfaction
Recognition
Promotion
Responsibility
Self-respect
Excitement

All these values relate to two things: looking after yourself and helping others. Often we pay too much attention to the first and not enough to the second. Does this apply to you? The truth is that purely selfish behaviour will make you less happy. You can really get a buzz out of putting others first! Break free, take control of your life, and find the values that can make you and your relationships with other people happier.

PEACEMAKER NO 2: BE AT ONE WITH YOURSELF

This occurs when your body and soul are in total harmony. Your conscience is clear, you are spiritually fulfilled, and everything is right with the world. The values we have just talked about are vital in achieving this state of well-being. There are also several other things you can do:

● *Relax and exercise* Exercise generates endorphins which relax you and are your body's natural painkillers. Enjoy aesthetic pursuits which make you feel emotional, like music.

● *Put things into perspective* Don't turn minor problems into major ones.

● *Beware of automatic thoughts that distress you* Ask yourself if they are rational, and if not laugh them off. If you can't, a good way of losing an unwanted thought from your mind is either to do something active or shut your eyes and just listen to every sound around you. Relaxation also helps because automatic thoughts are more likely to come when you are tense.

● *Reflect occasionally* Quiet moments of reflection and contemplation are great ways of re-charging your spiritual batteries. Question things if they are wrong. Blind obedience and apathy are the enemies of happiness.

● *Don't expect too much of life* Don't be greedy and you won't be disappointed. Remember a Dutch proverb, 'A man needs many things, but he can live with just a few.'

PEACEMAKER NO 3: ACCEPT THE PAST, LIVE FOR TODAY AND LOOK TO THE FUTURE

Don't live in the past and dwell on past successes or personal disasters. Have no regrets. Avoid thoughts such as 'I wish I'd done that' or 'What I might have done if ...' We all have skeletons in our cupboards, but make sure you don't open the door to let them haunt you. Confront your failures, be positive and ask yourself, 'How can I transform this liability into an asset?' The first step in doing this is to avoid blaming yourself for your failures. Come to terms with any guilt you may have. Put your mistakes into perspective – they're almost certainly not as important as you think and probably temporary in their effect. Seek forgiveness from the people you have wronged, and from God if you're religious. Then ask yourself 'What did I do wrong and what can I do to make sure that the same thing doesn't happen again?' To address this question successfully, learn from your past mistakes and think about your successes. Ask yourself 'What did I do right, and how can I use this expertise to good advantage in the future?' Concentrate your attention on the things that you can change. As the prayer at the end of each Alcoholics Anonymous meeting says, 'Give me the courage to change the things I can change, to accept the things I can't change and the wisdom to know the difference.'

Once you've come to terms with your past, live for the moment. Treat every day as special and try to make it as happy as possible. Make plans for the future, but don't let them destroy your enjoyment of the present. Now is always the best time to do something. Just listen to the story of Peter for one moment. Peter ran his own business and worked virtually all the time. 'I'm building a future for my wife and two children,' he said. 'I'm working so that I can afford to spend more time with them when the children are a bit older.' But he never did, because he was so hooked on his work. He never had enough time to enjoy the company of his family. Peter then lost everything he *really* cared about, when they walked out on him. Don't make the same mistake as Peter. Don't mortgage your present for your future in pursuit of a dream that might not prove so important after all, or may be unattainable.

PEACEMAKER NO 4: SPIRITUAL LIBERATION

This is just as important to peace of mind as it is to creativity. It is the feeling of spiritual liberation you get when you feel you're in total control of your life. You are living the life *you* want to live, not one that other people want you to live – just like in the film *Shirley Valentine* where Shirley re-discovers herself on holiday in Greece. Here is a step-by-step guide to achieve the same sort of liberation that Shirley felt:

1 ***Look at yourself*** Ask yourself, are you using and developing your talents to the full?
2 ***Question your routine*** Are you doing things automatically without thinking? Do you need to do them in that way, or are they really necessary at all?
3 ***Scrutinise your relationships*** Are you being taken for granted? Are people using you? What can I do to make them treat me as a real person and give me the love and respect I deserve?
4 ***Take a leap in the dark*** Have the courage to do what you've always wanted to do. Give yourself a break from your routine. Force your friends and loved ones to re-assess their relationship with you. If you always look after the children, take a day off and let your partner do it. He (or she) will soon find out the problems you face, and it will force him or her to become more understanding.

Just keep reminding yourself of the proverb 'A contented mind is a perpetual feast'. Peace of mind is the cause of lasting happiness, so go for it!

One Final Comment

Aristotle once wrote, 'If the eye were a living creature, sight would be its soul.' The key to a peaceful and stress-free life lies within you. A passion for spiritual purity will produce the tranquillity which the world cannot give. Care for your soul and you care for your future.

9

GET YOURSELF NOTICED BY THOSE WHO REALLY MATTER

This chapter will show you how to:

► *Improve your oral and written communication skills*

► *Speak your mind without offending people*

► *Successfully conduct and take part in meetings*

► *Read and use body language in order to give an impression of quiet confidence and efficiency*

► *Dress for success – how first impressions can make or break your career chances*

► *Mix with the right people*

► *Use humour to your advantage*

FILM STAR MERYL STREEP doesn't always get the parts she wants easily. When she enquired about the leading role in *Sophie's Choice*, she was turned down. She pleaded for an interview with the director and her dazzling performance got her the job. It pays to be noticed by the people who matter! But do you ever feel invisible? Do people walk by you as if you weren't there? Do you have difficulty making your presence felt with the right people? If so, read this chapter! Its main message is that to get noticed you will have to *sell yourself as a wonderful human being*. To do this you must obviously communicate effectively with other people. So read the principles of good communication below.

25 Ways To Communicate Better

Good communication must inspire people to do things for you. To do this you must remember the following:

COMMUNICATOR NO 1: POWER TO TOUCH HEARTS AND MINDS

'We shall fight on the beaches, we shall fight on the landing grounds ... we shall never surrender.' Churchill's famous words in 1940 turned a despondent Britain into a nation of all-conquering heroes. You, too, can have the same power to touch people's hearts and minds by preserving your integrity and empathising with those to whom you are communicating. *You must communicate concern.* You must be believable, yet use words, sometimes extravagantly, to capture people's imagination. Let your words shout out and take people's breath away! To gain your audience's attention, ask a provocative question or make a startling statement.

COMMUNICATOR NO 2: CONCENTRATED COGENCY

The story of the creation was told in 800 words in the Bible. Abraham Lincoln's Gettysburg Address, one of the most effective political speeches ever, was spoken in only three minutes. Communication is more powerful if it is cogent and concise. The secret is to be brief but compelling and convincing. Collect and then select information to focus on the key issues. Delete any unnecessary words, sentences, and phrases. For example, say 'usually', not 'in the majority of cases'. Also avoid warm-up paragraphs – you should get to the point straightaway. Your first sentence should hit people between the eyes and concentrate on the most important issue. Read the first sentence in any news story and you'll get the idea.

COMMUNICATOR NO 3: BEAUTY IN SIMPLICITY

When American Supreme Court Justice John Marshall Harlan said in 1896 'Our constitution is colour-blind', everybody instantly knew what he was talking about – a simple phrase conveyed so much meaning. This is what you should be trying to do in your communications. Don't over-complicate your language. Use plain English, avoiding clichés, jargon and unnecessarily long words. Keep your sentences as short as possible – lengthy sentences are a sure-fire way to lose your audience's attention.

Divide your writing into short sections with headings or sub-headings – break up a paragraph which is longer than 12 lines. Don't get bogged down in unnecessary detail – it reduces the impact of your message and makes it more difficult to find out what you are really trying to say and do. Write as you speak – 'I'm' 'I'll', 'I've', etc. Avoid phrases like 'and/or'. Use abbreviations as little as possible – too many can cause confusion.

COMMUNICATOR NO 4: MIRACLES FROM METAPHOR

Metaphor has always been a potent weapon in the armoury of the inspirational communicator. Think of the parables of Jesus and authors throughout the ages like John Steinbeck: 'In the souls of the people the grapes of wrath are filling and growing heavy, growing heavy for the vintage.' This one sentence summed up the anger and economic injustice for some people in the America of the Depression. Use metaphor in your communications to explain difficult concepts.

COMMUNICATOR NO 5: PASSION FROM CONVICTION

Make sure you have the urgency and conviction to deliver your message with passion and enthusiasm – have a mission to inform! Speak up for the truth, but do it with sensitivity towards the needs, opinions and feelings of your audience. Martin Luther King vehemently attacked racism, but he did it in a way that inspired whites as well as blacks. Stand up for yourself – give yourself moral support by being clear about your reasons for communicating something and by using appropriate body language. When talking to someone defiantly, keep your back straight and maintain eye-to-eye contact. Also slow, deep breathing will help to relax you. But *don't* attack people – this generates heat not change in their behaviour.

COMMUNICATOR NO 6: WALK THE TALK

Remember that actions speak louder than words. Your communication will be more powerful if you practise what you preach.

COMMUNICATOR NO 7: LEND YOUR EAR

Listen to what people have to say. Here are some effective listening tips:

- **Don't interrupt** Listen to what the other person has to say and wait patiently!
- **Keep relaxed** Tension and self-consciousness can distract you.
- **Get excited by and interested in what the other person is saying** If the conversation is boring, introduce a subject that is interesting to you, or simply force yourself to be interested! Ask questions and seek points of clarification.
- **Think about the consequences of not listening**
- **Don't do something else** Give the other person your undivided attention. *Appear* to listen as well as actually listen!
- **Listen to what is said, not how it is said** Don't be distracted by the person's idiosyncrasies or sex appeal! Listen to what is being said even if he or she is explaining it badly. Don't fall for the salesperson's patter!
- **Enjoy a busy and productive life** If you are active you are more alert and so a better listener. In conversation you can keep your mind more active by trying to anticipate the speaker's next point and critically questioning and summarising what is being said.

COMMUNICATOR NO 8: REMEMBER THAT GOOD COMMUNICATION IS A TWO-WAY PROCESS

Let other people communicate easily with you, and give them help so they can find their own solutions to their problems. Give people constructive feedback, encouragement and praise. Compliments should be sincere, as short as possible, spontaneous and specific. For example, avoid 'That was a good speech' – instead say 'That was a powerful speech, which changed my views on the subject entirely'. If you are on the receiving end of a compliment, don't belittle your performance – say thank you and smile rather than 'It wasn't that good really'. If you say it, people will start to believe it.

Make sure any criticism of someone is specific, constructive and given when the person is not tired or upset. Make comments relevant to the present and the future – there's no point going over past mistakes. Try not to be overly critical – concentrate on the most important problems. Try to anticipate responses to your criticism. Get all the facts, so that you can answer back with confidence! Criticise behaviour, not the person, and say what changes you'd like to see. Make sure you discuss the issue and work out a joint solution with the person concerned.

COMMUNICATOR NO 9: BE ACCURATE!

Always be factually and grammatically correct. Find facts to support your opinions, because intuitive feelings are not enough. Continuously learn in your own life so that you have the knowledge to communicate with authority. Remember author C.P. Snow's advice: 'Comment is free but facts are sacred'. Never reply to a communication (verbal or written) without all the information at your fingertips. Talk straight, honestly, and to the point. Don't be afraid of someone's reputation – you must say what needs to be said, whatever their position and whatever the potential consequences. So be brave – people will respect you more for sticking to your arguments and beliefs. Be precise in your language too. For example, don't say 'as soon as possible', but 'do it by tomorrow'.

COMMUNICATOR NO 10: BE PROMPT!

Richardson Sheffield, owned by the Australian company, McPherson's, is probably the most successful manufacturer of cutlery in the world. Its Laser knives have been market leaders for a long time. One of the reasons for this success has been the speed of its communications. The company has three inflexible rules: 1. Answer letters within the day; 2. Answer telexes within the hour; 3. Supply samples within 48 hours. Being prompt in your communications not only pleases people but also deals with issues when they are fresh in everybody's minds. Strike whilst the iron is hot!

COMMUNICATOR NO 11: USE TECHNOLOGY WHEN IT'S THE EASIER AND QUICKER OPTION

Computers, word processors, fax, electronic mail, telephone and teleconferencing (conferences by video) have all made communication quicker and easier. Exciting recent developments have been pocket computers and multimedia software that combines words, pictures, sound and video in a single presentation. The Internet, which makes it possible for computers to exchange messages and information worldwide is revolutionising communications. It allows people to exchange messages and large volumes of data.

Technological aids like these are useful, but they are there with one purpose in mind – to improve your communication systems. Ensure that they don't make you avoid essential face-to-face communications – it's not always easy to talk about problems over the telephone. The chances are, however, that technology will solve many of your communication problems. Voice-input computers, which recognise your own voice, are already on the market and soon will become cheaper and even better. You will be able to speak into the computer and it will be able to type what you say!

One computer expert from Silicon Valley has predicted that there will be at least as much technological progress in the next 12 years as there has been in the past 12. For example, CD-ROMs (compact discs for computers) are now available with as many as 2,000 books on them from which information can be easily accessed. You will still use the telephone more than anything, though, so here are some tips to use it well:

- Plan what you are going to say while you're waiting for the other person to answer.
- Plan complicated calls in advance by writing brief notes.
- Find out what the caller wants at the start of the call. This directs the call to its desired purpose as soon as possible.
- Deal with important matters first so that if the call is cut short you won't miss anything vital.
- Keep general chit-chat to a minimum and to the end of your conversation.
- Remember the telephone is better than a letter or memo because of the immediate response.
- Allocate a telephone time every day to do all your calls – this is more economic on time than doing them intermittently throughout the whole day. Try to ensure you won't be interrupted during this time.
- If someone doesn't answer, leave a message with somebody else, if no reply is necessary. Otherwise state when you are available to answer a return call.
- Use a secretary to screen your calls, if possible.
- Don't be afraid to say you are busy and will ring back later if you receive a call at an inconvenient time.
- Pull the plug out sometimes for a bit of peace – remember the telephone is a big time waster.
- Listen sympathetically to the other person's problems. It has been estimated that 87 per cent of business contacts are first made over the telephone. Always be courteous and respectful.
- Take notes or messages during a call if necessary, so have a pen and piece of paper handy.
- Return calls promptly.

COMMUNICATOR NO 12: THINK ABOUT COST AND TIME SAVED

Use the cheaper, alternative method of communication if it is just as effective and quick. Seek information to use your communication systems better, e.g. from the Post Office or computer companies. Use telephones and faxes at the cheaper times, if you can. Don't waste time trying to find someone to talk to, if it's not necessary. Experts estimate that more than half of all telephone calls are made to convey information that requires no response from the person being called. So leave a message on a person's electronic mail or answering machine, or with someone in the office.

COMMUNICATOR NO 13: DRESS FOR SUCCESS

First impressions can either make or break you, so how you look is extremely important. Research shows that appearance accounts for 55 per cent of the impression created, voice for 38 per cent and what you actually say a mere 7 per cent. So dress as though you mean business. Dress either formally or informally to suit the occasion, but always look smart. Make sure you look just as good in jeans as in a suit. So watch your diet – those extra pounds will always pop out somewhere where you don't want them!

Power dress by making sure that everything you wear (including make-up and hairstyle) matches and is co-ordinated. You must feel confident with your appearance, so dress in a way which suits you as well as other people. You must feel physically and mentally comfortable in your clothes. If you're self-conscious about them, you won't be at your best. Use a style that works for you and stick with it. Don't be afraid to look stunning – there's no such thing as a plain person, only one who chooses to be. There is no virtue in being anonymous. Finally, here are some grooming tips for when you are on the move:

● Remember that your whole appearance should reflect well on you, from your hairstyle right down to your shoes.
● Always have a spare of important clothes – shirt, blouse, briefs, tights (neutral and dark), etc.
● Don't forget the toiletries, make-up kit, jewellery and razor. Remember that pale, pearly nail polish is more flattering than bright red, because it is less likely to show chips.
● Carry an emergency sewing kit.

- Don't forget formal shoes and clothing for evening use.
- Prepare for photograph sessions – women should wear heavier make-up than normal, and make sure your hair is clean and shiny. Just think how US President Bill Clinton's wife, Hilary Clinton, transformed her image by changing her appearance.

Always look good and walk tall. Then you can take on the world and beat the pants off it!

COMMUNICATOR NO 14: USE HUMOUR TO YOUR ADVANTAGE

Groucho Marx said in the film, *Duck Soup*, 'Why, a four-year-old child could understand this report. Run out and find me a four-year-old child. I can't make head or tail out of it.' Such humour can make your life at work so much easier. It turns potentially embarrassing situations into totally agreeable ones. The use of humour also entertains, relieves tension and does wonders for your image. Remember you're not a stand-up comedian, though – perpetually cracking jokes will distract from the seriousness of your message. View humour as only one weapon in your communications armoury, not the complete artillery! But how do you get a laugh? Gene Perret, Bob Hope's joke writer for 20 years, has a few tips for the effective use of humour:

- Build and use a comedy collection, 25 jokes or stories that you find funny.
- Look for humour all the time, from your experiences and joke books.
- Be self-deprecating; humour which deflates your ego wins more friends than anything.
- Adapt your material to your comic style and the needs of the audience – be as topical and specific as you can. For example, Perret kept some fast food franchise managers happy by saying: 'McDonald's has sold more than 75 million hamburgers. They know, because they're on their fourth pound of mince.'

- Don't cause offence; when in doubt about any potentially insulting humour, leave it out.
- To drive home an important point, put the joke after it.
- Have a back-up line if nobody laughs – e.g. 'my wife said that wouldn't get any laughs'.
- Keep your material short, and tell the joke slowly. As Polonius said in Shakespeare's *Hamlet*: 'Brevity is the soul of wit.'
- Don't laugh at your own jokes while you're telling them.
- Practise! The more jokes you tell, the better you'll get at it.

Finally, remember there are ways to be humorous without telling a joke – quotes, cartoons, analogies and observations of what's going on around you.

COMMUNICATOR NO 15: SPEAK WELL IN PUBLIC

Research shows that managers think oral communications are more important than written ones. So public speaking skills are a number one priority, but it is still something which scares a lot of people rigid. Actress Patricia Hodge has said, 'Public speaking or opening a fête absolutely terrifies me, because it unmasks me.' These fears can be overcome by observing the following rules of good public speaking:

Rule 1: *Keep it brief* Remember what somebody once wrote about speaking: 'Keep It Short, Stupid' (KISS). Don't forget another wise observation, 'An after-dinner speech should be like a lady's dress: long enough to cover the subject and short enough to be interesting.'

Rule 2: *Understand what you are talking about* Learn everything you can about a subject before you start speaking about it. This not only gives your speaking confidence but also gives you the ability to deal competently with any questions after the speech.

Rule 3: *Talk with passion, enthusiasm and excitement* Talk about something you really believe in – an audience will sniff out any half-hearted hypocrisy. Be as informal as you can. If the speaker shows excitement about his or her subject, this will rub off on the audience. They will say to themselves: 'There must be something in this, if this guy can get so worked up about it.' Impact will also be lost if you fluff your opening and closing lines, so practise them like mad beforehand. Write the first and last line on a card as a memory aid.

Rule 4: *Entertain, but don't let this distract from your message* Tell jokes, but preferably do this at the beginning of the speech before you start on the serious content. Any further humour should be used to illustrate or underline the points you want to make. Remember that your audience wants to hear your views, not your jokes. Vary your voice – monotonous tones will send anyone to sleep.

Rule 5: *Focus on four or five key issues* The audience can't take in or remember long check lists. So keep the structure of your talk as simple as possible. Be selective about the key points you want to emphasise and repeat them for reinforcement. Research shows that people only remember less than 25 per cent of a speaker's ideas.

Rule 6: *Use visual aids to illustrate not dominate* Visual aids such as videos and overhead projector slides (OHPs) should not take over your speech but be used to make your message clearer and more compelling. Points on OHPs should be very brief and centred around the key issues mentioned in Rule 5. The audience will not cope with large amounts of detail – a slide with too much information is very daunting. Cards with key points are also a good memory aid. Do check before the talk that all the visual aids you need are available and the audience can see and hear them! For an important presentation it is worth considering employing a professional company to do some colour overhead projector slides. Look under Audio-Visual Services in your Yellow Pages.

Rule 7: *Remember the audience* Put yourself in the shoes of the audience. Respond to their interests and avoid talking directly against their prejudices – be subtle. Always emphasise the potential benefits of your message to the audience. Win their hearts and minds. Don't read out your speech, as this gives it less impact. Illustrate your points with examples, anecdotes, and vivid imagery – transport your audience into the situation you are talking about. Use phrases like 'imagine that ...'

Don't talk too fast, use pauses for impact and repeat the important points to lodge them in the audience's memory. Welcome questions and feedback – they are the only way to find out how good your talk really was. A speaker should also outline the objectives of the talk very early on, so that the listener can prepare to receive the information. Don't be too inflexible though, as you might have to change the talk a little to satisfy the audience's requirements. It may be a good idea to spend more time on a subject that particularly interests them.

Rule 8: *Remember what counts is your ability to get the audience on your side* Your talk's most important objective should be to change your audience's behaviour. So don't do anything to destroy trust with the audience, like getting flustered when things go wrong!

Rule 9: *Move around and maintain eye contact* This keeps people's attention better than somebody standing in one place. Extravagant hand gestures can also captivate an audience. Studies have found that speakers who avoid eye contact are viewed as insecure, dishonest and not interested in their audience.

Rule 10: *Practise and relax!* There is no substitute for it – either do public speaking or practise in private. As Mark Twain said, 'It usually takes no more than three weeks to prepare a good impromptu speech.' Slow deep breathing will calm you down before the big event. Even the best public speakers are nervous before a presentation. In fact, you should be worried if you don't have butterflies – they help to improve your performance. The key to successful public speaking, however, is not showing that you're nervous. So don't tell the audience you're nervous, and avoid any irritating nervous mannerisms. See yourself on videotape and you will find out why.

Finally, remember again the findings of psychologist Albert Mehrabian's research, which revealed that our impressions of a speaker are formed by 55 per cent of what we see (posture, gestures etc), 38 per cent by the voice we hear and only 7 per cent by the words used.

COMMUNICATOR NO 16: KNOW YOUR AUDIENCE AND EMPATHISE WITH THEM

You must always aim to satisfy your audience's needs when you are communicating. You need to empathise with them, i.e. view your communication through their eyes. Here are some tips to put this empathy into action:

- **Don't think of yourself** Communicate to inform your audience, not to protect your own interests.
- **Don't bore your audience** Entertain as much as you can and use simple, varied and lively language. Say sales 'jumped', for example, rather than 'increased' 20 per cent last year. Use a *Thesaurus* to increase your vocabulary.
- **Don't over-complicate** Keep your sentences short, and write as you speak.
- **Involve your audience** Relate to your audience's experiences with examples, anecdotes and research evidence. Start sentences with 'you' e.g. 'You make this organisation great' not 'This organisation is great'.
- **Dispel any doubt about your arguments** Speak and write powerfully, and back up any opinions with facts. Argue your points in a logical order. Start with the most important issues and identify the problem before providing solutions.
- **Remember the audience are busy people** Provide a statement of a problem and its solution as briefly and clearly as possible. Every report should have a summary of its key recommendations and conclusions. Use headings and sub-headings, graphs and tables for clarity.
- **Don't offend people** Know people's opinions, values and prejudices so you don't violate them. Give the bad news first in a sentence containing both good and bad

news. For example, 'I can't help you, but I can put you in touch with someone who can.'

● *Emphasise the benefits of your message* It should help your audience become more effective people. Clarify your objectives – begin a report or presentation with its aims, and give it a title which clearly reflects its purpose. Use 'Re' headings for memo's and letters which specifically state what they are concerned with. Always explain the reasons for your communication.

COMMUNICATOR NO 17: KNOW THE ART OF GOOD CONVERSATION

Are you sometimes lost for words in conversation? Then read these eight rules to improve your conversation style:

Rule 1: *Care about the other person* Someone once wrote, 'A gossip talks about others, a bore talks about himself, and a brilliant conversationalist talks about you.' Show genuine concern and interest in what the other person is saying. If you are in danger of being bored, ask questions or change the subject to something of more mutual interest. If you know whom you are going to talk to beforehand, find out their interests and prepare a few questions about them. There is nothing more flattering than someone who is interested in what you like and – even better – knows something about it. Never dwell on a subject the other person finds boring. Don't be pompous, self-opinionated or arrogant and never think you necessarily know better than the other person.

Rule 2: *Start a conversation well* There are six ways you can do this:

a Talk about the other person: 'Where do you live?'
b Talk about yourself: 'I live next door.'
c Talk about the situation you're in: 'It's warm in here, isn't it?'
d State a fact: 'I've just been to Paris for the weekend.'
e State an opinion: 'You look beautiful tonight.'
f Ask a question: 'What sort of music do you like?'

The best approach is probably to talk about your situation first, then follow it up with a question about the other person.

Rule 3: *Smile!* Practise smiling while you speak and while the other person is speaking. Believe it or not, there are several ways you can warm yourself up for smiling before an important conversation, according to authors Philippa Davies and Phillip Hodson:

a Chew vigorously – this warms up your smile muscles.
b Say 'Me … You' repeatedly in private – this improves your facial mobility!
c Massage your cheek muscles.
d Blow and shake your cheeks and lips like a horse sometimes does!

Rule 4: *Ask lots of questions* Open questions which require more than a 'yes' or 'no' answer are best. For example, 'What do you think about this report?' rather than 'Do you like this report?' Also avoid leading questions, if you want to find out someone's true opinion on something – don't say 'This report is rather good, isn't it?'

Rule 5: *Maintain eye contact* This communicates confidence and enables you to read the other person's reaction to what you're saying.

Rule 6: *Keep one step ahead of the other person* Try to anticipate questions so that you are better prepared when they come.

Rule 7: *Don't be overawed by the other person's status* They are human just like you! Don't forget any points of etiquette you need to follow, however. If in any doubt, be formal rather than informal.

Rule 8: *Look relaxed* Don't be hurried. Give yourself time to pause and breathe evenly when talking. Use slow, deep breathing to relax before an important conversation. Smile and watch your body language. Don't twitch or fiddle, hunch your shoulders or cross your arms and legs defensively. Don't talk too loudly or too softly – loudness is intimidating and quietness reflects timidity. Avoid being self-conscious – people will be paying little attention to your shortcomings.

COMMUNICATOR NO 18: KNOW HOW TO BREAK BAD NEWS

We all have to do this sometimes – someone dies, someone is made redundant and so on. How you deal with these situations at work is vitally important. Bad news travels fast, and a botched up interview can not only upset the people concerned but also badly affect the morale of their co-workers. So prepare yourself thoroughly. Have all the information at your fingertips, so that you can deal confidently with any questions. If a redundancy has been made according to a set procedure, know that procedure backwards. Try to justify the decision in your own mind. If you can't, maybe it's time to change jobs yourself. Don't blame anybody else for the decision – you are representing the organisation, so you can't pass the buck.

Most of all be empathetic. Always look at the problem through the eyes of the injured party, and communicate the bad news as quickly as possible to scotch any misguided rumours. Avoid Friday afternoon meetings, because the person will have the whole weekend to worry without any support or advice. At the interview be clear, concise and direct. Then sweeten the pill by giving any good news such as redundancy terms. If you know the person, be informal; otherwise be more formal. This makes the decision business related, and not a personal attack.

Use your own experience, or ask other people, to anticipate how the aggrieved person is likely to react. Then you can plan to do something about these eventualities beforehand. Just calmly accept any verbal abuse, or encourage the person to talk, when silent. Be understanding. See the person in private, except where a complete work group is to be made redundant and then a group meeting may be appropriate. Generally, however, privacy is the major requirement, so that the person is not embarrassed when becoming angry or upset. Be honest and open about the reasons for the decision. It will not be accepted if it is not fully understood. Be sincere, but don't apologise so much that you appear weak and indecisive. Use independent counsellors and outplacement agencies, if necessary.

COMMUNICATOR NO 19: LIKE (NOT LOATHE) MEETINGS!

'Meetings, bloody meetings!' How often have you said this in your working life? Meetings are often very frustrating and a big time waster, but they needn't be. There's no reason why you shouldn't like meetings if you do the following:

- *Make sure the meeting is absolutely vital* Try other forms of communication if they will do. Remember meetings are very labour intensive, because they involve a lot of people over quite a long time.
- *Set a meaningful agenda* Discuss issues which people think are important and which need to be discussed by *all* the people present. Every person at the meeting should be clear about its objectives and identify with each of the items on the agenda. Avoid making meetings too large and unmanageable. The agenda should contain enough information to describe exactly what will be discussed and what decisions need to be made, so that people can do some preparation before-hand.
- *Make everyone at the meeting feel important* Those present need to feel that they have the power to contribute to decisions made by the committee. It is particularly frustrating to speak at meetings and feel that nobody will listen or act upon what you say.
- *Pick the right chairperson* The chairperson needs to keep the meeting to the agenda and the scheduled time, and also facilitate discussion. But watch out for professional windbags who speak because they like the sound of their own voice. A good idea at a small meeting is to pass around a talking stick, normally a pencil or pen. A person

can only talk if he or she is holding the stick or it is in the middle of the group. It minimises interruptions and forces people to listen and reflect upon what other people are saying. It really does work!

● *Watch the time*   Effective meetings start and finish on time, so allocate time for each item on the agenda. It is a good idea to schedule meetings to finish at 5 o'clock, then people won't be tempted to go over the time allotted.

● *Take minutes*   To record decisions made and proposed actions for the future it is vital to take accurate notes.

COMMUNICATOR NO 20: USE INFORMAL COMMUNICATION CHANNELS

The grapevine, canteen and social occasions are all a good opportunity for a gossip. This can be a powerful form of communication, so managers must ensure that people are well informed and rumours are scotched early on.

COMMUNICATOR NO 21: BE SEXY WITHOUT BEING SEXIST

You can't escape the power of sex appeal when dealing with other people, particularly in first-time encounters. Raymond Chandler once wrote, 'She gave me a smile I could feel in my hip pocket.' You don't have to be overtly sexy (skimpy clothing can give the wrong messages) but lay on the charm, which is more dependent on your personal integrity than your appearance. So avoid being sexist – it is offensive.

COMMUNICATOR NO 22: ANTICIPATE ANY BARRIERS BETWEEN YOU AND YOUR AUDIENCE

Bureaucracy may get in the way because there are too many levels of management. Mistrust, geographical location and lack of time can also hinder effective communication. Management style is also important. If you don't involve people in decision making, they will be less likely to respond enthusiastically to a communication. If you don't listen, two-way communication becomes impossible. Poor presentation is the final obstacle to good communication. This can be caused by too much detail, over-reliance on a certain medium (e.g. lecturing rather than using visual aids), the irrelevance of the material given, and linguistic difficulties. Misunderstanding can be caused by jargon and different uses of language – between the board room and the shop floor, for example.

COMMUNICATOR NO 23: COMMUNICATE WITH THE PEOPLE WHO MATTER

Know who they are, and go out of your way to communicate with them. Sit next to them at meetings, in the canteen and so on. Don't be afraid to ask for things.

COMMUNICATOR NO 24: ENCOURAGE SPECIFIC AND POSITIVE ACTION

Be precise to encourage prompt action, and, for example, say 'do that by Friday' not 'do this as soon as possible'. Use direct language. Avoid phrases like 'tends to', 'perhaps', or 'maybe'. Prefer positive words to negative ones, and be aware of the negative impact of words like 'problem', 'delay' and 'impossible'. People genuinely respond better to what they can rather than what they can't do. Communicate constructively to change behaviour, not to express anger. Say: 'Your work hasn't been up to your usual standard recently, is there anything I can do to help?' rather than 'You have a problem with your work.'

COMMUNICATOR NO 25: USE BODY LANGUAGE TO YOUR ADVANTAGE

We have mentioned the power of body language throughout this chapter, but here are some additional points:

- **Become aware of body language** It's easy to miss if you're not looking out for it.
- **Folded arms reflect defensiveness.**
- **Eye contact reflects openness and trust** If you have difficulty maintaining eye contact, look from eyebrow to eyebrow and then down to the mouth (but not further), and then back to the eyebrows again. But you should still look the other person in the eye occasionally, because the other person will notice what you're doing!
- **Firm handshake** This usually reflects a decisive person.
- **Passiveness** This is shown by avoiding direct eye contact, keeping the chin low, folding the arms across the chest, standing unbalanced and looking uncomfortable.
- **Aggressiveness** Gestures like clenched fists, pointing the index finger, hands on hips, a hard stare and a chin held high all indicate aggressiveness.
- **Use mirroring to your advantage** This means your gestures are subtly the same as those of the person you're talking to, without mimicking. This can allow you to relate to people better.
- **Think before you touch someone** Use touch as a gesture of warmth and concern, but be careful. It can also be seen as intrusive, demeaning or seductive.
- **A smile can win a thousand hearts** See communication principle 17 on page 108.
- **Watch your dress, grooming and hairstyle** They say a lot about you. Be smart and dress according to the situation, see communication principle 13 on page 101.
- **Spot a liar** When people choose to lie during a conversation, they will often suddenly cross their arms or legs as an advance self-defence against challenge. Research also shows that liars are less likely to touch or sit very close to you. They may avoid eye contact, or sit on the edge of

their chairs as a sign that they would like to leave. Liars also reduce the number of their hand gestures. They will often clench their hands into a fist, thrust them into their pockets or clasp them firmly together. They will touch their faces, noses, ears and chins more. Also watch out for their speech – a liar's voice becomes less confident and more monotonous. Research also shows that liars talk less and make more mistakes in their speech. By the way, if you are lying and the other person tugs at or rubs his or her earlobe, you have been seen through!

● **Watch people's posture** To be most effective when speaking in public adopt an open stance, in which the palms are open and your weight is evenly balanced. When sitting, don't slump or sprawl across the chair. To look assertive have an upright posture with relaxed hands and appearance, a confident voice and a responsive facial expression. Finally, Jane Lyle in her book *Understanding Body Language* (Chancellor Press, 1993), says watch out for the following gestures (their meanings are in italics).

a Rubbing hands vigorously – *pleasurable sense of expectation or satisfaction.*

b Slow rubbing of hands – *warning signal for a con.*

c Scratching the head – *confusion, doubt, uncertainty.*

d Both hands behind the head – *superiority, confidence and possible arrogance.*

e Hand clasping back of the neck – *trying to control angry feelings.*

f Hand stroking or chin rubbing – *your ideas are being given careful consideration.*

g Head resting on, or being supported by the hand – *boredom or fatigue.*

h Hands clasped lightly on the cheek – *analysing and evaluating what you are saying.*

i Hand resting lightly behind the back – *extreme confidence.*

j Steepling (fingertips and thumbs are pressed together forming a triangle) – *confidence, or (if the head is tilted back at the same time) arrogance.*

k Clenched hands when speaking – *what is being talked about is frustrating.*

l Clenched hands when listening – *the listener is responding negatively.*

m Arms folded with thumbs pointing upwards – *nearly impossible to convince.*

n Lightly scratching or rubbing the side of the neck with one or two fingers – *insecurity, unfamiliarity, or thinks you are a liar.*

o Hiding the thumbs inside the fist – *difficulty in analysing a problem*

p Hands pressed together as in prayer – *a desire to persuade or underline a point gently but firmly.*

q Separating the little finger from the rest of the fingers – *possible eccentricity and a strong sense of individuality.*

One Final Thought

Research shows that your relationships with other people make you happier than anything else. What greater incentive could there be to communicate better?

10

INFLUENCE PEOPLE

This chapter will show you how to:

▶ *Get people to do things for you*

▶ *Improve your selling and negotiating skills*

▶ *Deal with your boss and other people you meet at work*

▶ *Deal with problem people and defuse potentially explosive situations*

▶ *Develop friendships at work that will help you in times of trouble*

▶ *Be a good team player*

▶ *Understand people from different cultures*

WRITE DOWN who has had the biggest influence on your life. Then think of the reasons why. Is it their integrity? Compassion? Faithfulness? The list could be quite long, but the message of this chapter is that you can learn a lot from your personal relationships to help you influence people at work. Four ways of doing this will be discussed:

Win respect By being true to yourself, and your values.

Make people your friends Through developing long term, committed relationships at work.

Be a good team player How to get the best out of people in work groups.

Persuade people How to sell and negotiate.

116

If you remember these four things, you will be able to hold your head high, because you know you are influencing other people's lives for the better. So let's begin!

How To Win Respect

If your boss demoted you, would your colleagues at work still look up to you? Is your authority solely dependent upon your position, or do you have the power to influence people, however lowly your circumstances? You will only have such power if you win people's respect. Here are some tips to help you do this.

RESPECT WINNER NO 1: BE TRUE TO THE RIGHT VALUES

Follow the advice of Polonius in Shakespeare's play, *Hamlet*: 'To thine own self be true'. Live by your values and beliefs, but do so pragmatically. How you interpret them may have to change with every new experience. For example, love is a great virtue but you can't put others first all the time. You have got to think of yourself sometimes, so that you have the physical and mental capacity to help others. Being true to yourself means defending *your rights* just as much as other people's. As Confucius once said, you need to be loyal to yourself as well as considerate of others.

RESPECT WINNER NO 2: KNOW YOURSELF TO KNOW OTHERS BETTER

When you look in the mirror, do you see the real you or a pale imitation? Don't kid yourself – beware of self-delusion. Realistically assess your strengths and weaknesses, so that you can build upon your strengths and work on or avoid your weaknesses. Self-analysis is always difficult, however, and often painful, but you must reveal and scrutinise the real you if you are to be successful. Think of all the different areas of activity in your life and make a list of your good and bad points. Be brutally honest – if it doesn't hurt, you aren't being honest enough. Then ask yourself the following questions: 'How can I use my strengths to my advantage?' 'Can I exploit any opportunities in the world around me?' 'How can I turn weaknesses into strengths?' 'If I am stuck with them, how can I minimise their effect on my life?' 'Are there any threats in the world around me (e.g. a new boss) and can I do anything about them?'

RESPECT WINNER NO 3: RETURN GOOD FOR EVIL

Revenge won't do your reputation any good in the long term, and it will also increase your blood pressure. It creates bad feeling and will make your relationship with the person concerned very difficult. Stand aloof as much as you can from office politics, cliques and gossip. Just be true to yourself and stand up for what you believe in. Most of all care about your relationships with other people – be compassionate and kind, give cheerfully, be honest and keep your promises. Don't be hypocritical either. Don't be arrogant and pompous. In short, keep your integrity even when other people are losing theirs.

RESPECT WINNER NO 4: USE YOUR TALENTS TO THE FULL

He was born Thomas John Woodward in the humble Welsh mining valley of Treforest over 50 years ago. He burst into the big time with his hit single 'It's Not Unusual'. His name was Tom Jones. Jones' ability to win the hearts of millions has come from using and developing his talent. You could do the same, if you know your strengths and use them effectively, learning from experience and striving for continuous improvement. Never be satisfied with mediocrity and always aim for excellent standards.

Don't indefinitely postpone what you've always wanted to do with your life. Get out of a rut! Go for a bright new future, but make sure it isn't a false one. You need to be aware of the likely problems as well as the advantages. You may be going out of the frying pan into the fire, as many people discover when they set up their own business (see Chapter Fourteen). But remember life should be a challenge, not a painful experience. Don't look back at the end of your life and say 'I wish I'd done that'. As pop legend Bob Dylan once said, 'What's money? A man is a success if he gets up in the morning and goes to bed at night and in between does what he wants to do.' Do what *you* want to do, not what somebody tells you or expects you to do. Achievement in life means making the most of what you've got, and happiness comes from achievement. Doing something useful is the passport to a truly happy life.

RESPECT WINNER NO 5: STAY COOL IN A CRISIS

There are ten ways that you can keep your head while everyone else is losing theirs:

- *Use humour* Laugh and joke about any situation as much as you can – humour drains away anger.
- *Don't be a fool and rush in* Wait a bit before doing anything. Give yourself time to reflect and work out the best solution to a problem, but don't procrastinate.
- *Relax* Breathe slowly and deeply to calm yourself down. You will then think more clearly.
- *Remember it could be a storm in a teacup* Don't attach greater importance to something than it really warrants. You then won't get so worked up about it.
- *Don't rush around* Keep your physical movements to a minimum. Running around aimlessly will only wind you up.
- *Think courageous defiance* Think defiantly as much

as you can in every situation. Read books about courageous people and draw inspiration from them.
- **Empathise** Understand the views of the people in
dispute so that you understand their problems and are
better able to find solutions to them.
- **Hold your head up** Always give the impression of
calm assurance in public, even when your stomach is
churning inside. Cry in private but make sure the door is
closed.
- **Quietness within** If you are at peace with yourself,
you are more likely to be at peace with the world.
- **Keep optimistic** Believe that no problems are insurmountable. Concentrate on solutions, not obstacles in
your way. Over-analysis of the obstacles may so daunt you
that you can't do anything.

RESPECT WINNER NO 6: FULFIL YOUR DREAMS

The year was 1963. The city was Liverpool. The group was
The Beatles. 'I Want to Hold Your Hand' sold over a million
copies before it was even released. There were minor riots in
many cities. Within a few months, the Beatles had the top
five singles in the USA pop charts. Beatlemania was at its
peak. John, Paul, George and Ringo had fulfilled their
wildest dreams. Can you learn any lessons from the success
of The Beatles? They made the most of their talent, perse-
vering through the early days of obscurity, starting with John
and Paul's fateful meeting at a church dance in 1957. They
had terrific love and enthusiasm for what they were doing.
They show you that the fulfilment of dreams can make you
happy and admired.

People win respect when they get results, particularly
against the toughest of odds, by doing something constructive and useful with their lives. They set challenging goals for
themselves and achieve them through positive thinking,
willpower, courage and determination. They can change the
world in their own way. You could do the same, if you are
clear about your life's purpose and how to achieve it. Enlist

the support of family and friends. Sort out the difference between the possible and impossible – be realistic but don't be overly cautious and unambitious.

RESPECT WINNER NO 7: PASS YOUR TESTS OF CHARACTER

There will be moments of truth in your life, which will make or break your potential. This is what faced Jesus in the Garden of Gethsemane, and Martin Luther King at the start of his civil rights campaign. King received a call around midnight, threatening to kill him and his family. His resolution to do what was right saw him through this crisis. You can do the same.

How To Make People Your Friends

Real friends help you in bad times as well as good. But how do you inspire such loyalty at work? Here are some tips to help you have lasting friendships.

- *Think the same about things that really matter* Real friendships are based on common objectives and values. When talking to people, emphasise the things on which you agree. Try to get as many 'Yes' responses as you can.
- *Think and listen friendship* Speak words of appreciation and demonstrate gratitude in thoughtful ways. Show interest in what other people are doing. Think before you speak, and express your feelings without hurting other people's. Put yourself in their shoes and see their point of view. Accept them for what they are – warts 'n' all!
- *Never go to sleep angry* Avoid resentment, bitterness, jealousy, envy, and thoughts of revenge. Don't blame others when you are at fault. Be slow to anger –

stay cool when dealing with difficult people. Don't hold grudges, and be as patient as you can.

- **Forgive and forget** Forgive and show mercy in your relationships. When dealing with an issue, attack the problem, not the person. Compromise rather than issue an ultimatum. Acknowledge the strengths of people before you address their weaknesses. If you have to criticise someone, do it with sensitivity and understanding of his or her problems, and don't go out of your way to find faults in people.
- **Loyalty** Be faithful to others in bad times as well as good. Loyalty should not be blind, however. Don't follow someone if you think they are wrong.
- **Give yourself time to grow** Make time for yourself so that you are in better shape to give time to others.
- **Put yourself out** Nothing is too much trouble for a friend.
- **Think long-term** The friendships that really matter are long-term relationships. If you take advantage of someone you will lose out in the end, even though you might gain in the short term.
- **Make 'em laugh!** A sense of humour is always an asset in any relationship.
- **Beware of stereotyping people** Don't be put off by someone just because you associate them with a group of people you are not keen on. Meet people with an open mind and not preconceived ideas – fight your prejudices.
- **Give people your time** In this hurly burly world it is easy to rush around everywhere and be oblivious to the needs of others. Make time for other people. Show concern and avoid apathy and indifference. Be interested in what they are doing. Treat them with respect, humility and humanity. Build up their self-esteem and express your appreciation of them. Remember that true friendship is unconditional. Accept the responsibility to help people in good times or bad. Encourage them.
- **Treat everybody the same** Every person is a human being with feelings, so act accordingly. True friendship has no class or ethnic barriers.
- **Trust people** Give them responsibility and confide in

them. Jointly decide things as much as possible, and always involve people in the decisions that affect them. You need to ask yourself several questions if you are to successfully involve people in this way:

a ***Does the person want it?*** People may resist the responsibility that involvement brings, because they have always been told what to do. In these circumstances, communicate the benefits of successful involvement and change people's attitudes through training and development.

b ***Have you assessed the importance of the issue being considered?*** People will want to become more involved, when they think that something is important.

c ***Have you used all appropriate methods of involvement?*** Try informal chats or group meetings.

d ***Have you obtained a consensus view?*** People will be more committed to a decision if they feel they have had some impact upon the final result.

● ***Honour people's rights*** Everyone has a right to privacy and independence. You won't win any friends if you attempt to make people dependent on you. People will like you more if you help them to become more rounded human beings. Friendship doesn't mean making someone into something they aren't and moulding them into your own image. With help, everyone has the ability to solve their own problems. Treat other people's problems as confidentially as you can, though – if information has to be passed on, openly say so.

● ***Communicate with openness and consideration*** Be as open as you possibly can, but argue in private. Be considerate and courteous. Use little phrases like: 'I'm sorry to trouble you', 'Would you be so kind as to …', and always give reasons for your actions or behaviour.

● ***Never lose your integrity*** Be sincere in your relationships, and have a genuine interest in the other person's situation. Be impartial in your judgement. Don't be hypocritical.

● ***Motivate people*** People are more likely to be friendly if they are motivated and happy at their work. Remember the following six key points for successful motivation:

a Design jobs to satisfy people's needs – giving people autonomy, the chance to use their skills, security, self-esteem, money and fulfilment from doing something worthwhile. Make work fun!

b Involve people in setting the targets they are expected to achieve.

c Ensure that the targets are demanding but achievable.

d Give people a realistic idea of the link between their performance and the reward they could get for it.

e Reward people effectively. Rewards should be seen by them as desirable, whether they are financial, or non-financial factors like job satisfaction, training and education or social activities.

f Give people regular and constructive feedback on how they are doing.

● ***Don't waste other people's time*** Do things with them in the quickest possible time.

● ***Treat everyone like a million dollars*** You meet lots of people at work – your boss, colleagues, problem employees, and people from outside bodies like trade unions, pressure groups, and government. The key to successful relationships with these people is your attitude towards them. Put yourself in their shoes and see their point of view. Never ask somebody to do something you would not do yourself, and never exploit or manipulate anyone.

Give people your time and treat them humanely. Make your relationships with them more personal by referring to them by name. Treat each person as if they were the last person on this planet, and you were dependent on them for your survival! If this doesn't work (and it usually does), accept your rejection with grace and be philosophic about it. You can't please all of the people all of the time, but you can please most of the people most of the time. To help you do this, let's look at two important situations: handling a problem person, and dealing with people from different cultures.

How To Handle Your Problem Person

Relationships with your boss or colleagues can be a big headache. So here are some tips to deal with a problem person.

- *Don't disagree in public.*
- *Empathise* Listen to the person's problems. Show understanding and concern. Give support when necessary.
- *Be positive and confident in your discussions* Stick to what you believe in. Never compromise your values or professional integrity. Don't be defensive. Give considered opinions and disagree politely.
- *Take the initiative* If something is wrong, go and talk about it. Ask what the problem is, be positive and suggest solutions. It could well be that without realising it you are partly at fault. Talk about issues, not personalities. Expose an attack immediately and try to draw the venom from it. For example, say: 'That was a serious accusation, did you really mean it that way?' Force the other person to be specific. For example 'Why do you say that I'm incompetent?'
- *Don't lose your cool* State your opinions assertively, but without losing control.
- *Don't take personally comments which are made in the heat of the moment*
- *Exploit the person's weaknesses*
- *Nip any potentially explosive situations in the bud* Keep an eye on what's happening in your department or section, particularly on any grievances bubbling underneath the surface. Resolve these problems early and show people that you understand – be the peacemaker. Eliminate resistance to change by making it attractive through getting people to see its benefits. Involve them in the implementation of the change, so that they feel a greater sense of ownership and responsibility towards it. Learn the history of relationships between people in your

section, so that you can do something about possible personality clashes.

However hard you try though, some heated confrontations do take place. In this situation be the mediator who tries to get both sides to see each other's point of view, and the arbitrator who settles the dispute by finding an agreeable compromise. After the argument make sure that the two opposing sides part on friendly terms. Remember they have got to continue to work together!

- **Don't be totally revealing about your personal life at work** This is inappropriate and can be damaging.
- **Break unnecessary rules if they hinder your relationship with other people**
- **Remember the person's five unspoken requests** (according to American author Warren Smith):

  a Hear and understand me
  b Even if you disagree with me, please don't make me wrong
  c Acknowledge the greatness within me
  d Remember to look for my friendly intentions during disagreements
  e Tell me the truth with compassion

- **Don't embarrass the person**
- **Keep the person informed** Decisions can then be made without causing you problems. Also keep yourself informed to deal with any difficult questions.
- **Don't lie or brag**
- **Try disarming humour** When faced with sarcastic criticism, laugh and say, for example, 'The compliments are coming thick and fast today!'
- **Get the person to sit down if you can** It's more difficult to be aggressive when sitting down.
- **Help the person to regain control, if he or she is exploding**
- **Don't be tempted into an endless argument** Concentrate on finding out what is the right thing to do and whose opinions are correct.
- **Swallow your pride and boost the other person's ego** Give people the impression that they are more

knowledgeable than you, even if they are not. Show your agreement with the things they have said that you think are right. Don't pretend to be a better person than you really are. This will only make people eager to see you fail. If you do something wrong, admit it and be prepared to apologise when necessary.

- *Offer a reward in return for a change in the other person's behaviour* You could say: 'I'll correct my mistakes, if you tell me clearly and quietly what they are.'
- *Know your rights* Make sure you know your job description and terms and conditions of employment so that someone can't ask you to do something you shouldn't be doing.
- *As a last resort use your organisation's grievance procedures and enlist the support of your trade union or professional association* You should record the nature, time and place of any verbal abuse, and keep any written documentary evidence such as notes or memos.
- *Respect your boss's decisions, even if you do not agree with them* This applies even if your boss is the problem.

How To Deal With People From Different Cultures

The European Union (EU) and the globalisation of markets have brought people from different countries into much closer contact. You will have to understand them as well as you can, if you are to influence them. The best thing you can do is speak in their own language and follow the normal standards of good behaviour like integrity, courtesy, and politeness. You also need to be aware of their likes and dislikes. The following examples are taken from John Mole's book *Mind Your Manners: Managing Business Cultures in Europe* (Nicholas Brealey, 1995).

AMERICANS People from the USA value hard work, business, self-help, liberty and justice. Opinions range from right wing – sometimes racist – views through to people who have views very similar to the British Labour Party. But there is a popular view that individuals should run their own lives with as little interference as possible from the government. Americans like people who aggressively pursue their goals and strive for success. They are heavily influenced by the pursuit of excellence, competence, professionalism and Christian values. They are also highly pragmatic – nothing is valid unless it is useful.

BELGIANS They are divided into two communities, Flanders (which speaks Flemish, and includes Antwerp) and Wallonia in the South (which is French speaking). There is a great deal of antipathy between the two groups. Brussels, although in Flanders, is 75 per cent French speaking. There is a weak sense of national identity. People consider themselves Walloons or Flemings first, Europeans second and Belgians last. Both communities value compromise, negotiation and conservatism. They are reluctant to accept new ideas if the old ways will do. They can, however, laugh at themselves. Flemings are very sensitive about speaking French, so use another language first!

BRITISH You will greatly irritate people from Scotland, Wales and Northern Ireland if you call them 'English'. The south east of England is more individualistic than the rest of Britain, which is more community minded. Traditional British characteristics of politeness, modesty and restraint are also very important, but American-style aggression has become more common since the 1980s. British culture is anti-business, especially outside the south of England, but this is changing as the country becomes more desperate for new jobs. Britain is still a class-ridden society – 'the old school tie', your background and how you speak are important although becoming less so. Performance is now the major requirement for success. The British are passionate about the things they hold dear – television, the National Health Service, the welfare state, the monarchy, gardening, football, cricket and any activity which is challenging and exciting. Britain's poor economic performance has been caused more by poor management and under-investment in research and development, training and education than by the motivation of the workforce. The British aren't lazy! They are also less formal than foreigners believe – first names and humour are often used. To start a conversation with a British person, talk about the weather! Like the Americans, the British are pragmatic in their thinking.

DANES These people value honesty and meticulous punctuality highly. They are plain speaking and dislike snobbishness, ostentation and the outward trappings of success.

DUTCH The Dutch dislike pretension, deviousness and ostentation – if you have money, don't flaunt it. They are hard working and often take work home. They speak plainly and directly.

FRENCH They are combative in meetings and will often shout you down, so don't be afraid to shout back. They also have a passion for food and wine, and believe that there is more to life than work. Hard work is admired, but workaholism is not. Holidays, work-free weekends, sport, cultural activities and family life are all considered very important. If you are talking to a French person, therefore, don't talk about work all the time! Also avoid personal remarks, however friendly or amusing they are meant to be, because they will be seen as rude and aggressive. At work humour is rarely used at meetings or on formal occasions – it is seen as flippant. The French are also obsessive about the correct use of language. You will have to use the mother tongue more than in any other European country, because English is not so well spoken. This is changing, however, as French children now start to learn English at the age of seven. 'Intellectual' is not a term of abuse as it is in some countries, like Britain. The French enjoy abstract thought and theory. They can also be very stubborn and inflexible when confronted with change, if it isn't seen to be logical.

GERMANS They will take the most conservative option, if given a choice. This comes from a strong fear of insecurity and an uneasiness with uncertainty. They are deferential to people in authority, and will rarely contradict or criticise their bosses. So relationships with them are often distant. They look for strong, decisive and competent leaders and managers. Outbursts of anger are seen as undesirable and a sign of weakness. Germans are extremely punctual, competitive, ambitious and don't sympathise with failure. They value success and its outward trappings, and being seen to work hard is important. People give total commitment during office hours, but they don't like to work at home, unless it's absolutely vital. German men are often chauvinist! Germans also value their privacy very highly, and are more formal in their relationships at work than either the British or Americans. They don't like strangers to joke with them, and humour is kept out of the workplace.

GREEKS They prefer face-to-face communication to writing or the telephone. They welcome foreigners with outside ideas, but don't try to exploit or dominate them! There is little discimination against women. Humour is a vital part of Greek life, both at work and outside it, but don't be pretentious. If you are negotiating with a Greek, beware when he or she becomes quiet and withdrawn. It means that things aren't going well. Most people start work early and finish at lunchtime, but larger companies are changing to British working hours.

IRISH As on mainland Britain, Irish people are concerned with the problems of Northern Ireland only if they are directly affected by them. The IRA is not widely supported, and the Roman Catholic Church still has a very important influence. The Irish value personal relationships and humour, but steer clear of religion and politics, until you know an Irish person really well! They also dislike pretentiousness and anything which restricts individual freedom and improvisation, like rigid systems and bureaucracy. Beware when negotiating with them though, as their outward amiability is combined with astuteness and often stubbornness.

ITALIANS   They value inventiveness, imagination, intelligence and education. Don't be afraid to quote renowned thinkers of the past and present. They tolerate inefficiency and genuine mistakes, but hate arrogance, rudeness or deliberate lateness. They like people who look good and are good conversationalists without being overbearing. They love life and rarely take work home.

JAPANESE   Unlike in the West, the group has superiority over the individual. So the Japanese value co-operation, sharing responsibility, intensive discussion and a fanatical devotion to the good of the organisation and the groups within it. Great emphasis is given to seniority and experience. Confrontation is avoided if at all possible, and so the Japanese are extremely polite, deferential, and sometimes appear vague and indecisive. They also put the company before even the family – *karoshi*, death by overwork, is a problem in Japan.

LUXEMBOURGERS   They generally use German as their business language, but speak the mother tongue at home. They are also fluent in French. They like people to be reserved and modest, not assertive.

PORTUGUESE   They like personal and informal relationships and are very competitive.

SPANISH   They like to make decisions on their own, so meetings are avoided wherever possible. They value character and breeding higher than cleverness. It is expected for people to show off their wealth through their car, clothes, etc. Business and special relationships are informal and friendly. For example, at a business lunch, work is not discussed until the coffee arrives. Spaniards also value modesty (rather than assertiveness), personal pride (rather than technical ability), procrastination and humour.

How To Be A Good Team Player

Here are some tips to influence people when you are working in groups:

- **_Identify with the common purpose_** All effective groups have common objectives which are shared by all their members. So be enthusiastic about achieving these goals and communicate this enthusiasm to the other members of your group. Make sure that the group has a vision for the future which will inspire it to do great things. Remember that maximum commitment will only be given by individual group members if their values are consistent with group objectives and they perceive some reward from contributing to the group effort.

- **_State your views but be prepared to listen to other people's_** What you want may not necessarily be what is best for the group. So give other people time to speak and don't interrupt them. Make sure that everything said is relevant to the task in hand, and use each group member's experience and ability.

- **_Use your strengths and avoid your weaknesses_** To be effective in a group you should concentrate on the tasks you are best at. Are you creative, with lots of ideas? Are you a visionary who strongly influences the group's future policy? Are you good at getting things done? Do you have an eye for detail? Do you have the specialist knowledge required? Do you motivate other group members to do things? Are you a good chairperson? Are you a good summariser? Do you listen to other people? Are you good at settling disputes between group members? If you can't do some of these essential jobs, then somebody else in the group will have to! The best group is one where its members have complementary skills and different areas of specialist knowledge. This is why cross-functional teams including marketing, finance, production and personnel specialists are particularly creative and effective.

- **Trust your other group members**   If there is no trust within the group its members won't co-operate effectively because they are suspicious and unwilling to share their ideas. Trust can be increased through the group doing things together socially or in outdoor training courses.

- **Be willing to help the group effort**   Try to understand the other group members' opinions and needs. Help them to find solutions to their problems. Encourage them to participate in discussion, and if they are reluctant to be in the group, convince them of the benefits of being a group member. Group discussion is not a stage to show people what a wonderful person you are, but a means of getting the best possible performance from the group.

- **Make sure the group is the right size**   Between five and eight members gets the best results in most cases. Anything less and you won't have enough skills and knowledge to draw on. Anything much bigger and the group will be unmanageable. It will be more difficult to involve each group member, and cliques may form. Many people are less willing to contribute in a large group.

- **Forget about your status and position in the hierarchy**   What counts is the performance of each individual group member. Don't pull rank for the sake of your ego!

- **Seek feedback**   Someone from outside the group must occasionally judge how it is performing in terms of achieving group tasks and satisfying the needs of each member. The group must also monitor its performance so that continuous improvement can be achieved.

- **Beware of 'groupthink'**   Groupthink is when people won't challenge even the most foolish of ideas or decisions for fear of threatening the group itself. A classic example of this was the CIA's disastrous invasion of Cuba in the Bay of Pigs in 1961. To avoid groupthink be self-critical, open to outside ideas and challenge conventional wisdom.

How To Negotiate A Good Deal

Here are some tips to make you a better negotiator:

- *Be assertive* Know what you want and stick to your guns until a compromise is reached. Never show any sign of weakness or wavering! Learn to say no and be firm.
- *Empathise and listen* Look at the negotiation from the other person's point of view. Show your concern, and ask yourself 'What can I do to help?' Listen intently to what the other person is saying. Sweeten the deal with things that aren't particularly important to you but could be important to the other person. But don't be soft and feel sorry for the other person. You will both be trying to get the best possible deal.
- *Do your homework* Make sure you have all the facts at your fingertips before you start negotiating. Try to anticipate what the other person is likely to want. Assess beforehand the strengths and weaknesses of your negotiating position, so that you can play to your strengths and keep the discussion away from your weaknesses.
- *Stay cool* Always stay calm and never lose your temper. Try slow, deep breathing to relax you before the negotiating starts. Step back from an emotional outburst by the other person by saying, for example, 'Let me think about it'. See such outbursts as opportunities for counter punching.
- *Be persistent* Consistently repeating your negotiating position will reinforce your message and stop the discussion drifting away from the central issue.
- *Be concise* Keep your points short and simple.
- *Don't be afraid to ask* Ask for clarification if necessary. Obviously you must fully understand the other person's position. Use periodic summaries to gain agreement in certain areas. For example, ask 'Are we agreed on this, so that we can move on to the next point?'
- *Offer a compromise* Remember that refusing to compromise may get you nothing, because the other

person may back out of the negotiation altogether. Try to create a win-win situation where both sides achieve their objectives. Get the other person excited about side issues that aren't really important, and make concessions reluctantly. Remember that the overriding aim of any negotiation is to reach agreement, not to score debating points or boost your ego. Always bear in mind three possible levels of settlement during your negotiations:

a the best possible deal
b what you expect to get, based upon a realistic assessment of the circumstances
c the worst deal that is still acceptable to you.

Avoid discussing differences of opinion, and concentrate on points of common interest and possible agreement. Don't be greedy, and don't accept an ultimatum.

- *Think before you say 'Yes'* Don't rush in to accept the deal and then regret it later. Give yourself time to think it over.
- *Be patient* Never rush the person you are negotiating with.
- *Don't talk too much* Protracted silence can be very effective when negotiating.
- *Attack the problem not the person* Don't be insulting or aggressive, but give your energies totally to resolving the issue under negotiation.
- *Negotiate backwards* Work out in advance where the other person would like to end up.
- *Be as honest as you have to be* Don't lie – you're finished if the other person finds out you are not telling the truth. Reveal all the information necessary for the negotiation, but keep one or two trump cards up your sleeve for critical moments.
- *Say how important the issues are to you* This is particularly effective, when things are going badly for you.
- *Encourage the other person to speak* This will reveal weaknesses in the person's arguments and give away information that is valuable to you.

- *Read coded messages* For example, 'I can't accept this as it stands' probably means 'Some of your proposals are acceptable but others will have to be changed'. 'I'll let you know' may mean 'Sorry, I'm not interested', or 'I need time to think it over'.
- *Close the deal as quickly as possible* Move quickly to clinch a deal, as soon as the outline of an agreement becomes clear. If the conclusion is delayed, people may begin to have second thoughts.
- *Don't forget your future relationship with the other person* Remember that driving too hard a bargain may sour future relations with the other person. So there may be times when you have to accept less to preserve a good long-term relationship.

How To Become A Super Salesperson

Here are some tips to sell your ideas and opinions more effectively to other people.

- *Believe in what you are selling* Persuasiveness comes from integrity rather than deceit. If you cheat people, they will eventually find out and never trust you again. So always sell something which you can believe in.
- *Negotiate well* The skills you need to negotiate are also important when you are selling. So re-read the section above.
- *Never take no for an answer* Be persistent in the face of people's refusal to accept your ideas.
- *Communicate well* The ability to write and speak well is obviously essential to effective selling. So have another look at Chapter Nine. A sense of humour is particularly important in selling.
- *Be open with people* Talk about the potential problems as well as the likely benefits of what you're proposing. This will show people you have thought through your ideas successfully.

- **Be confident but not cocky** Believe in yourself, but remember that arrogance is a big turn-off.
- **Show calm assurance** Give the impression you have complete mastery of the ideas you are trying to sell, so get as much knowledge as you possibly can!
- **Remember whom you are talking to** The more knowledgeable and educated people are, the better prepared you will have to be.
- **Give people an offer they can't refuse** Make sure that the benefits of your ideas are as appealing as possible.
- **Do something special for the other person** Find out what people want and do everything you can to satisfy them. The personal touch is vital. Show concern for them and be interested in what interests them. If you really want to impress them, do something for their children.
- **Know when to back pedal** Don't push an idea down someone's throat, if they're not ready for it yet. Try at a later date, when the situation has improved.
- **Deal with objections politely** Don't lose your patience over objections which you think are illogical, incorrect or stupid.

One Final Thought

Actress Joanna Lumley has said the most sacred thing we have is 'to be our own person'. This is the best way to influence people. Be true to yourself and your values and you will win the lasting respect which will make people do things for you.

11

BE A GREAT MANAGER

This chapter will show you how to:

▶ *Become a great manager in the quickest time possible*

▶ *Assess your strengths and weaknesses as a manager*

▶ *Have a successful managerial career and still have a happy personal life*

NO ONE could forget the faces of the starving Ethiopian children on our television screens in 1984. Millions of hearts were touched, but only a few did anything about it. One of them was of course Bob Geldof, the founder of Band Aid – a great manager, if ever there was one! He inspired people to do something about the famine in Ethiopia. He was successful because everyone could identify with the cause. Geldof also made sure that no one got lost in a vast bureaucratic organisation. Action through small groups was his successful formula, which is why he structured the formation of separate groups like Truckers for Band Aid and Builders for Band Aid.

Geldof managed from the heart and that's how you can become a great manager who inspires people. This chapter will show you how to do this. You need to touch people's hearts and minds to obtain extraordinary performance from them. In this sense every manager is a leader influencing the lives of other employees. So management is the same thing as leadership. This might surprise you. Writers on leadership, like Warren Bennis from America, tell us that leadership is something totally different from management. But look at the key characteristics of a leader; someone who:

a Defines a vision for the future and effectively communicates that vision so that people are committed to carrying it out, like Martin Luther King's dream of racial harmony.
b Develops people to make the most of their potential.
c Innovates through continuous curiosity and encourages creative thinking from others.
d Passionately cares about people.
e Inspires trust.
f Takes a long-term view.
g Challenges conventional wisdom.
h Always does what he or she thinks is right, even in the face of fierce opposition.

Shouldn't these also be the characteristics of great managers? They should do all these things for their section or department, just as much as the chief executive should do them for the whole organisation. The great manager is also not a boss. Think about this adapted message from writer Doris Lessing in her book, *African Laughter* (HarperCollins, 1992):

The boss drives his people,
The great manager inspires them.

The boss depends on authority,
The great manager depends on goodwill.

The boss evokes fear,
The great manager radiates love.

The boss says 'I',
The great manager says 'We'.

The boss shows who is wrong,
The great manager shows what is wrong.

The boss knows how it is done,

The great manager knows how to do it.

The boss demands respect,
The great manager commands respect.

So be a great manager,
Not a boss.

Do you have the qualities required by a great manager? Try this quiz.

Are You A Great Manager?

This is a quiz for either practising managers or people who want to be a manager. If you are in the latter group, imagine yourself as a manager and then ask yourself for each question 'Would I do this for the people I am responsible for?' You should count the number of your yes and no answers and then refer to page 198 for an analysis of whether or not you are (or are likely to become) a great manager.

1 Do you frequently observe, talk with and listen to your people?
2 Do you have a clear vision for the future of your department?
3 Does that vision inspire your people to achieve extraordinary performance?
4 Are you passionate and enthusiastic about what you are trying to do in your job?
5 Do you often discuss your people's objectives with them, so that they are clear about what they are?
6 Do you volunteer for jobs that no one else would handle?
7 Do you ask for feedback from more senior management?
8 Do you critically look at the style of management adopted by people in the senior or middle management positions you aspire to?
9 Do you seek management experience outside your

organisation through spare time work with a voluntary organisation or a professional body?

10 Do you continually analyse your strengths and weaknesses in management?

11 Do you trust your people?

12 Do you delegate?

13 Do you agree objectives with your people and then give them the autonomy to achieve them in their own way?

14 Do you make yourself available to talk over the progress of delegated projects?

15 Are you approachable?

16 Do you let your people learn from their own mistakes and help them pick up the pieces if necessary?

17 Do you question the need for established systems and procedures?

18 Do you reward good performance?

19 Do you give your people feedback?

20 Do you effectively communicate with your people?

21 Do you treat your people with empathy and understanding?

22 Do you help your people to overcome their weaknesses and any stress?

23 Do you socialise with your people?

24 Are you the same person at these social events?

25 Do you make every effort to make your people feel secure?

26 Do you make your people's jobs as interesting as possible?

27 Do you make it as easy as possible for your people to do their jobs effectively?

28 Do you always strive for excellent standards for yourself and your people?

29 Do you make clear to your people the standards that are required?

30 Do you praise good performance and react promptly to poor performance?

31 Do you ask what people need to do their job better and then act upon it?

32 Are you concerned about your people's training and development?

33 Are you punctual and enthusiastic?
34 Do you earn respect?
35 Do you keep your promises?
36 Do you let other people take the credit when your department is praised?
37 Do you stand up for your people in public, when they are criticised by those outside your department?
38 Do your people think you have the ability to manage them effectively?
39 Do you treat everyone the same?
40 Are you consistent with people?
41 Are you happy about the balance you achieve between work and leisure?
42 Have you the courage to make really tough decisions?
43 Can you think and act clearly in a crisis?
44 Are you prepared to lose popularity for what you think is right?

---

20 Ways To Become A Great Manager

MEGAMOTIVATOR NO 1: NEVER LOSE YOUR INTEGRITY

You don't have to be loved or even liked to be a great manager. But you must never lose your integrity, because, if you do, you will lose the trust and respect of your people. People will believe what you say if they believe in you. US General Schwarzkopf, victor of the Gulf War, is an inspirational leader because of his great integrity and warmth. But he is not especially liked by his officers because of his temper, which gave him the nickname of Stormin' Norman. The three principles of good management by which he keeps his integrity are given in his book, *It Doesn't Take a Hero* (Bantam Press, 1992), co-written with Peter Petre:

a Always be truthful.

b Never look down on the people who report to you.

c Have the courage to say no.

Some additional integrity preservers are:

- *Act with consistency and fairness* Treat everybody the same. Justice should not only be done but *seen* to be done. Don't say one thing and do the exact opposite. Remember the motto of Queen Elizabeth I: 'Ever the same'.
- *Don't have favourites* Be impartial in your judgements.
- *Keep your promises and honour your agreements.*
- *Be open with people.*
- *Speak up for the truth and encourage others to do the same* Don't distort the true situation to make yourself look better. Don't surround yourself with 'Yes-men'. Be prepared to suffer for the cause of right. Remember you can't please all of the people all of the time!
- *Understand yourself better* You can then work on your weaknesses before they lose you respect.

Robert E. Lee, the Confederate General in the American Civil War, was a hero even in defeat because of his integrity. His second-in-command, Stonewall Jackson, said he would have followed him blindfolded. People will do the same for you, if you keep their respect. Your integrity will give you the inner strength to manage successfully.

MEGAMOTIVATOR NO 2: SELL YOUR VISION

A great manager must have a customer-driven vision for the future and sell that vision, so that people work like mad to achieve it. For this to happen, a vision must be simple, clear and realistic; have no finish line so that your people can continually strive for it; and touch your people's hearts and minds. You need to be an effective communicator, especially orally, and the vision must be devoted to a worthy cause. Give your time to doing what your people think is worthwhile, and be seen to believe in your vision.

Such an ideal vision statement was made by Steve Jobs in 1980 for Apple, the computer company he co-founded, 'To make a contribution to the world by making tools for the mind that advance humankind'. Just as good is the vision of Disney, which is simply 'To make people happy'. If your people can identify with such a vision, they will move mountains for you. So never stop telling them about it.

MEGAMOTIVATOR NO 3: DO WHAT'S RIGHT

'Right makes might' as Abraham Lincoln once remarked. The great manager must not only do what is right given the situation but also be a force for good – remember that Hitler thought exterminating the Jews was the right thing to do. Clearly such attitudes de-motivate people through a lack of faith in what they are doing. So to inspire people you must do what is right, but bear in mind the following:

- *Stick to your principles* Be clear about the values which govern your behaviour, such as treat others as you would like them to treat you. Always question your values to make sure they are the right ones.
- *Listen to other people's views but remember you have the final responsibility* So don't be distracted by people who might oppose you.
- *Be decisive once you have considered all the facts and everyone's opinions* Don't delay or procrastinate. Be action-oriented!
- *Be sensitive to your people's needs* If you act decisively or even ruthlessly your people will accept what's happening, once they believe you understand them and have their interests at heart. Early on in his job as chief executive of ICI, Sir John Harvey-Jones had to make redundancies to ensure the long-term prosperity of the company, but they were accepted because those who lost their jobs were well compensated and treated well.
- *Have the courage to make the tough decisions* Moral courage and strength of mind will help you to

conquer any problem or difficulty. The great manager must be able to cope with challenge and controversy.

- **Be persistent** If at first you don't succeed, try and try again!
- **Accept responsibility** Remember the words that President Truman had on his desk: 'The buck stops here.'

MEGAMOTIVATOR NO 4: SEE YOUR PEOPLE

This is management by wandering about (MBWA), popularised by American management writers like Tom Peters. Be visible and don't lock yourself away in your office. Get in touch with your people – observe, praise and listen to them. Abraham Lincoln spent three quarters of his time meeting people to keep in touch with ordinary people's views. Sir Colin Marshall, when chief executive of British Airways, gave 300 presentations to groups of 100 employees to get his message of 'putting people first' across to 30,000 employees.

MEGAMOTIVATOR NO 5: BE COMPASSIONATE

You must show your people that you care. Understand them, be sensitive to their needs, and take them seriously. Remember that nothing or nobody is more important than your people. So prioritise your time accordingly. Give as much time as possible to each person, whether or not they have problems. But honour their privacy – don't pry into their private lives unless they want you to. Don't ignore or take them for granted, and pay attention to the small things because these might be important to them. People will react either positively or negatively to the way you treat them, so always give them reasons why you are doing something or asking them to do something. Discipline in private. Deal effectively with criticism, and never blame others for your faults. Be courteous, and give them hope for the future. As Napoleon once said, 'A leader is a dealer in hope.'

You must understand your people's problems, so doing their job for even a little while might be a good idea. Sam Walton, founder of the most successful retailer in the world, Wal-Mart Stores, was legendary for his concern for his people (whom he called associates). One night he couldn't sleep, so he bought some doughnuts and shared them with some of his associates at a local depot. He chatted with them, responded to them, and they loved it! All truly great leaders and managers have had this philosophy of all-consuming service to their people – Jesus, Confucius and Lincoln, for example.

In Point 3 above, though, we said that the great manager also has to be decisive and do things that people might not like. So great managers must be **tough but tender**, with the toughness to make the difficult decisions but the tenderness and kindness needed to understand their employees. If a manager tries to do anything without a kind heart, people won't understand it and therefore view it with suspicion and cynicism. If people are to be committed and love change, they must know that their manager is a compassionate person who has the courage to make the tough decisions.

MEGAMOTIVATOR NO 6: LEAD BY EXAMPLE

Remember that actions speak louder than words. Walk the talk! Always let people know what you are doing, and practise what you preach. Never ask anybody to do anything that you would never do yourself.

MEGAMOTIVATOR NO 7: DON'T BE TOO BIG FOR YOUR BOOTS

The great manager knows that real respect comes from good performance and being *primus inter pares* – first among equals. People who motivate others don't pull rank. A good, strong manager is prepared to swallow humble pie occasionally and accept that other people might have better ideas.

Employees must be taken seriously, listened to, and given the chance to answer questions such as:

a What would you do to make the department run better?
b How can I make your job easier and more interesting?
c Is there any job I should be delegating to you?

You don't have to be a grovelling Uriah Heep to be a great manager, but you do have to listen with humility.

MEGAMOTIVATOR NO 8: REMEMBER THE THREE Ss

These have been suggested as essential to good management by Jack Welch, the chief executive of the American company, General Electric:

a *Speed* The great manager must act fast, responding quickly to employees and customers.
b *Simplicity* The great manager loves doing things as simply as possible. Simplify your structure and systems so that work in your department can be done quickly, easily and effectively.
c *Self-confidence* If you lose confidence in yourself, people will lose confidence in you.

MEGAMOTIVATOR NO 9: BE WORTHY OF YOUR PEOPLE'S TRUST

Trust is vital to good management. If people don't trust you, they won't do great things for you. Research shows that ten essentials for creating trust are: availability, competence, consistency, discretion, fairness, integrity, loyalty, openness, promise fulfilment and sensitivity to people's needs. Franklin D. Roosevelt embraced all those things, and this is why he won the trust of the American people during the Depression of the 1930s. People really believed him when he said, 'I pledge you, I pledge myself to a new deal for the American people'.

MEGAMOTIVATOR NO 10: TRUE GRIT

The great manager has the courage to stand out from the crowd and a dogged determination to succeed even in times of extreme adversity. Never accept defeat – be resilient! Be ruthlessly self-disciplined. Nelson Mandela's determination and inspiration saw South Africa through the darkest hours of apartheid and gave hope to millions.

MEGAMOTIVATOR NO 11: NEVER BE TOO PROUD TO LEARN

The great manager realises the importance of lifelong learning and constant self-improvement. Seek as much management experience as possible, both inside and outside your organisation. Look for variety and learn from your leisure activities as well as your work. Continually analyse your strengths and weaknesses as a manager, building on your strengths and working on your weaknesses. Seek constructive feedback from those who matter – senior managers, subordinates and your family. Learn from adversity and your mistakes!

MEGAMOTIVATOR NO 12: STRIVE FOR EXCELLENCE

Thomas Watson Snr, founder of IBM, sought excellence in three areas:

a Give full consideration to the individual employee.
b Spend a lot of time keeping customers happy.
c Go to the last mile to do a thing right.

Like Watson, you must strive for excellence at work and never settle for second best. Be obsessed with success! The vision of General Electric boss, Jack Welch, is for every employee to *be excellent*, not just search for excellence. Sir John Harvey-Jones has also said that a business leader must have a passion for perfection. Walt Disney motivated his staff, continually prodding for perfection, communicating standards of excellence and encouraging people to achieve them. You do the same!

MEGAMOTIVATOR NO 13: ADAPT YOUR MANAGEMENT STYLE TO YOUR SITUATION

You will have to be autocratic when a decision has to be made quickly and decisively, but do this with your people's needs uppermost in your mind. A sensitive autocrat is much more effective than an insensitive one. Field Marshal Montgomery, victor at El Alamein, could be autocratic and sometimes ruthless, but his concern for his troops was legendary. As his biographer Nigel Hamilton said, he wanted to feel like a caring doctor, in touch with the pulse of his men.

On the other hand, you will have to be democratic and involve your people in any decision which is particularly important to them. People will not accept change if they have not been involved in bringing it about. The ideal is for people to discover for themselves what changes are required and then find their own solutions to any consequent problems. This is the essence of empowerment, which we shall discuss in Point 20 on page 152.

MEGAMOTIVATOR NO 14: TAKE ADVANTAGE OF YOUR PEOPLE'S STRENGTHS AND ANY LUCK WHICH COMES YOUR WAY

This means that you must find out what these strengths are. But the aim must always be to see your people grow as human beings. Remember the phrase 'grow people, grow profits!' Don't manipulate them. Sir John Harvey-Jones believes that manipulation (or the fear of it) causes more antagonism and resentment than almost anything else. Also accept good luck gratefully and use it to your advantage.

MEGAMOTIVATOR NO 15: GIVE YOURSELF TIME FOR REFLECTION AND THINK LONG TERM

It is so easy to become obsessed with doing things and immersing yourself in detail. Ex-US President Jimmy Carter even sanctioned the use of the White House tennis courts! If you get too bogged down in detail you will lose sight of where you should be going in the future. Give yourself time for reflection to do this. This will also enable you to get to know yourself better, so that you can discover the inner strength necessary to become a great manager. Plan reflection time into your week, and don't make excuses because you think other things are more important. They are not.

In the early days of the Second World War, Roosevelt worried some people by appearing not to devote enough time to it. He spent much time in his weekend camp, playing with his stamps. A devotee then responded to this by saying, 'Well, maybe he thinks'. Great managers, like Roosevelt, think long term. They don't just react to events, they plan ahead and try to anticipate the future. In particular, they know that their success is dependent upon building a long-term relationship with their people, which requires a long-term investment in them through things like training and education.

MEGAMOTIVATOR NO 16: GRAFT WITH A LAUGH

Great managers have the stamina to work extremely hard and effectively. They can also use humour to get out of difficult situations without offending anybody.

MEGAMOTIVATOR NO 17: BE A SOCIAL REVOLUTIONARY

John Adams, one of the Founding Fathers of America, said that the real American Revolution took place in the hearts and minds of every American. To be a great manager, you must also touch your people's hearts and minds, so that they rebel against mediocrity and second-rate performance. Question anything which stops your people doing this. Cut through red tape, if necessary. Take a clear ethical stance on the future of your department or organisation, which can inspire your people, like Anita Roddick, founder and chief executive of the Body Shop. Her concern for the environment is well known, and she has always supported the view that organisations should have a social purpose. So she decided to open a soap factory in a very poor area of Glasgow rather than near the company's headquarters in Sussex. Roddick has also made a virtue of flying in the face of business convention. She has said, 'I look at what the cosmetics trade is doing and walk in the opposite direction.'

MEGAMOTIVATOR NO 18: KEEP YOUR MIND AND BODY HEALTHY

Great managers have physical vitality, stamina and drive. They also have the capacity to control stress and strike the right balance between their work and leisure.

MEGAMOTIVATOR NO 19: ENCOURAGE CREATIVE THINKING AND LOVE CHANGE

Be open with people and invite dissent. Confront your people to generate new ideas, but do it compassionately. For example, have the ability to forgive mistakes and manage conflict and disagreement so that they are constructive and productive. Be a peacemaker, if necessary, and seek a consensus of opinion. Always question established systems and procedures, challenge the status quo, and encourage calculated risk taking. See and seize opportunities within agreed policies. Love change and get your people to love it, too, by making change a rewarding, non-threatening and challenging experience.

MEGAMOTIVATOR NO 20: EMPOWER YOUR PEOPLE

Empowerment is a much used phrase in management these days. But what does it mean? It involves giving your people power and control over the decisions which affect their jobs. They find *their own* solutions to problems which *they* have identified. You don't tell them they have a problem, they discover the problem for themselves. In short, empowerment means that people are in control of their own destinies at work. Obviously this has important implications for managers. Most important, they must get people to motivate themselves. There are a number of things that a great manager can do to achieve such empowerment:

- **Allow your people to find their own purpose**   They will be much more committed to what you as a manager are trying to do, if they can voluntarily identify with the vision for the future of your department. Your people must find their own purpose, but your job is to make sure that it's the same as yours! Great managers in the past have done this very successfully. Nelson, before the Battle of Trafalgar, only had to say 'England expects that every man will do his duty', and then his whole fleet knew what they had to do. Similarly all the England soccer captain, Bobby Moore, had to say to his team before the World Cup Final in 1966 was 'Let's go'. Another footballing legend, Danny Blanchflower, said about one of the greatest ever football managers, Matt Busby, 'He creates a purpose in life'. If you can do this you will have as great a team as Busby had.

- **Make your people feel like heroes**   If your people feel ten feet tall, they will have the confidence and self-esteem to do great things.

- **Only specify what to do, not how to do it**   Set clear jointly agreed objectives, but give people freedom to work out how to achieve them. Give people as much freedom as possible to decide how they work, where they work, and when they work. This is of particular importance to those with families, who need greater work flexibility.

- *Create a good team spirit* The empowering manager makes sure that people work well as a team. So, the manager must also be a good team player (see page 132). Creating small, self-managing work groups (like quality circles) are another good way of empowering your people.
- *Involve your people in decisions that affect them* This gives people ownership of the problems and issues facing them, so it becomes *their* responsibility to do something about them. But for this to happen there must be real involvement. In other words, listen to what your people have to say and act upon it. Don't just ask for their views, and then forget them. Your people will quickly see through such 'pseudo-democracy'.
- *Trust your people* Let people get on with their jobs without interference. If it is possible, let them work at home if preferred. Many people are much more effective at home than in the office. Trust also means delegating as much as you can.
- *Judge people on their results* Reward good performance, because people will obviously put more effort into their jobs if they are being adequately rewarded in terms of money, recognition and job satisfaction. Emphasise that it is the quality of their work which is important not necessarily the quantity. Encourage them to relax at work and outside it. Long hours can cause staleness and lower levels of productivity and creativity.
- *Hands-off management* Don't be tempted to over-supervise and annoy your people. Let them get on with it! The empowering manager is an enabler, guide, facilitator, teacher and coach. Create an environment in which your people can learn to solve their own problems. Listen and advise. Persuade rather than order people, and always make yourself available to talk over the progress of projects.
- *Remember that a good manager gets the best from people* The best way to judge a manager is by people's performance.
- *Be open and give people knowledge* Don't feel threatened by talented, knowledgeable people. Knowledge gives people the power to make the right decisions.

- *Let people feel secure* Fear is the biggest enemy of empowerment. Guarantee employment security if you can. Make people feel part of a big family which will help and encourage them.
- *Overcome people's fears* People might feel threatened by empowerment, because they are used to being told what to do. Such people must be persuaded of the benefits that empowerment can give them. So train them adequately!
- *Free people from bureaucracy* Reduce the levels of management so that people don't feel helpless and lost in countless levels of hierarchy. Also keep meetings to an absolute minimum and avoid unnecessary paperwork.
- *Let people grow as human beings* Encourage them to learn, train, educate and develop themselves to make the most of their potential.
- *Make people's jobs fun, exciting and rewarding* People will be more likely to motivate themselves if their work is fun and vitally important to them.
- *Give people the resources to do their jobs* Make sure that they have the necessary money, materials, equipment and any necessary additional personnel.

One Final Thought

Management writer Peter Drucker has said that management is about getting things done through the people. So the most important virtue of the great manager is humanity, and concern for employees. If they are aware of that concern, they will achieve the extraordinary performance that every manager is looking for.

12

KEEP YOUR
CUSTOMERS SMILING

This chapter will show you how to:

▶ *Know your internal and external customers
and their needs*

▶ *Satisfy customer needs through a committed
workforce, quality, innovation and
responsiveness to the external environment*

JUST THINK about the following statistics:

● Each unhappy customer will tell, on average, nine other
people.
● 96 per cent of all unhappy customers never complain.
● 91 per cent of those who complain won't come back.
● It costs five times more to win a new customer than keep
an existing one.

Your customers are important, so keep them happy! No
customers, no salary, and no organisation. Happy customers
will make your job more fulfilling and worthwhile. They also
enable your organisation to charge more for its product or
service and make bigger profits. If you forget your
customers, then they will forget you and take their money
elsewhere. So you must give your customers what they want.
As Polaroid believe, you must delight them and exceed their

expectations. This chapter will show you how to do this, but first let us answer an important question:

Who Are Your Customers?

They are not only the people who buy your organisation's product or service. They are also the people whom you work for within your organisation. These are sometimes called your **internal customers**. You have to provide them with the best possible service, so that they can do the best possible job. So apply what is said in this chapter to your internal customers just as much as to those who pay for your product or service.

How To Keep Your Customers Happy

REMEMBER THE CUSTOMER IS ALWAYS RIGHT

Every employee must truly believe this, or the customer won't get the best possible service. Stew Leonard, owner of one of the most successful supermarkets in the world, has two rules which his employees enthusiastically follow:

Rule 1: The customer is always right.
Rule 2: If the customer is wrong, re-read Rule One.

CREATE A WONDERFUL WORKFORCE

There are several ways you can create a workforce which is totally dedicated to your customers.

- *Have the right objectives* People will be more committed if they can identify with what your organisation is doing. So convince them that its objectives are really worthwhile by emphasising how it helps its customers. For example, before they do anything, employees of the following organisations should continually ask themselves:

  a But does it sell cars? (Ford)
  b But does it help children? (Save The Children Fund)
  c But does it help students? (A university)
  d But does it help to sell our product or service? (Your organisation)

Remember it is the thought of helping other people which really inspires people to do great things.

- *Effective recruitment and selection* Get the people who have the greatest potential for customer friendliness.
- *Good leadership* Top management and every other manager should set a good example with respect to customer service – they must never lose touch with what the customer wants. The best way to do this is to go out and meet them. Top managers should spend at least 25 per cent of their time in contact with their customers. The President of Hyatt Hotels in America worked as a doorman at the Hyatt in Chicago, and he learned more about his customers there in a day than in a month working in his office!
- *Treat people humanely* Satisfy your employees' needs, trust them, involve them in decision-making and be open with them.
- *Training* To give people the knowledge and skills required to serve the customer they must be well trained. Your customer service policy should be clearly communicated. Regularly remind people in informal discussions that the customer comes first. Never stop training them!
- *Make work fun and exciting* Happy employees mean happy customers.
- *Reward people for satisfying customers* Give them bonuses, fringe benefits and recognition. Don't forget to

treat people like human beings and say thank you!

- *Codes of Practice* These can be useful to ensure that employees deal with customers effectively and ethically.
- *Empower people* They will then satisfy customers without any prompting from management. This means trusting and openly involving people in decisions like the formation of your customer service policy. Allow feedback on the problems and the implementation of any such policy. Listen to what your people want and act upon their good suggestions. See page 152 for more detail on empowerment.
- *Keep on asking the $64,000 question* How can I make it easier for our people to satisfy our customers? This will involve improving your seven Ss ...

MAKE SURE YOUR SEVEN Ss ARE DRIVEN BY YOUR CUSTOMERS

The American management consultants McKinsey developed a 'Seven S Framework' which perfectly describes what you can change within your organisation to improve the service to your customers. The Seven Ss are:

1 *Strategy* Make sure all your policies put the customer first.
2 *Structure* Don't let bureaucracy get in the way of satisfying your customers. Reduce the layers of management, if necessary. Simplify your structure so that it is best able to carry out your customer-driven strategy. For example, don't automatically say: 'How can we increase the efficiency of our office? Say 'Do we need it in the first place to best satisfy our customers?'
3 *Systems* Improve how well you get things done in your organisation, including communication methods, and make sure that everyone has the information they need to do their job effectively. Don't think that computers will automatically increase the efficiency of your systems. People have to use them effectively first!
4 *Staff* Make sure you have a wonderful workforce.

5 **Skills**   Train people to ensure they have the skills necessary to satisfy your customers.

6 **Style**   Your management style must be sensitive to the needs of your employees and customers.

7 **Shared values**   Commonly called corporate culture, which is defined as the values and beliefs held by all employees. Everyone must really believe in giving the customer the best possible service. People must strive for excellence.

KNOW YOUR CUSTOMERS

You must get to know your customers better in four ways:

- **Empathise with them**   See the world through their eyes.
- **Listen to them regularly and carefully**   Make good use of customer contact. Also listen to others in the distribution chain, like suppliers and retailers, about how they think you can improve your customer service.
- **Socialise with them**   Arrange social events for some of your customers so that you can get to know them better and find out their views.
- **Do some market research**   You will need information about:

  a **Customers' needs and wants and their satisfaction with your performance**   Particularly in relation to your price, distribution, product, promotion and overall impression of customer service. Are they likely to buy your product or service again?

  b **Purchasing behaviour**   Who buys your product or service? Who makes the decision to buy it? Who uses it? Why do people buy it? How frequently do they buy it? How many customers do you have? How many of these are new since last year and how many have been lost? Who are the top 20 customers and what proportion of sales and profits do they account for? What is the average purchase per customer? Are the biggest customers the most satisfied ones?

  c **Your external environment**   Political, economic,

social and technological factors affecting your customers' tastes and preferences are important. In particular, you must find out your actual and potential competitors. What are they doing that will take business away from you? What are they doing badly that you can take advantage of?

d **Different market segments (or niches) and their customer characteristics** How can you split your customers up into different groups? You can do this by geographical region, age, sex, income, occupation, education, religion, race, social class, lifestyle, personality and stage in the family life cycle (under 35s, 35 to 64 year olds and older people, with or without children).

e **Gaps in home and overseas markets to be exploited.**

f **Changes in the size of your market** Are your sales rising, falling or stagnant? Is your market (at home or overseas) big enough for your organisation to make a profit?

g **Your future strategies and their impact on customers.**

Remember that *customer perceptions* of your product or service are vital to the success of your organisation. You must use market research to find out what these are, but there are dangers in being totally reliant on it. In the 1980s British Airways carried out some market research and found that business travellers wanted an 'on time, no frills service'. Then British Midland came along and gave them these frills: free drinks and newspapers, cooked breakfasts and so on. Customers so loved them that British Airways were forced to do the same and forget about their original market research!

LOVE YOUR CUSTOMERS

You may think that the word 'love' is a bit over the top, but it reflects the intensity of feeling towards customers required for success in organisations today. Here is what you can do to love your customers:

● **Customise** Make sure that your product or service

satisfies the needs and wants of every customer. Make sure that you provide a 'unique selling proposition'.

- **Treat customers like a friend** Be polite, courteous and prepared to do anything for the customer. Some organisations even send their customers thank you notes and Christmas cards. Be very conscious of first impressions. Make sure your employees dress and act professionally. Get them to smile a lot and talk with concern. Keep your promises to your customers, and be reliable. Bear in mind that you are trying to build a long-term relationship with your customers for repeat business.
- **Measure customer satisfaction frequently** Look at the number of complaints, and things that annoy or please your customers. Then do something about them!
- **Care for quality** Customers want the best possible quality at the lowest possible price. This is why total quality management (TQM) and the international quality standard ISO 9000 (formerly British Standard BS 5750), are so important in organisations today. The main beliefs of total quality are:

  a **living quality** Every employee should automatically think quality during every minute of his or her working day.

  b **zero defects** Getting it right first time, every time.

  c **continous improvement** Everyone should keep on trying to improve quality. This is the Japanese concept of *kaizen*.

  d **empowerment** Everyone should voluntarily act to improve quality in their jobs. They themselves should identify their work problems and find solutions to them. This is how quality circles work, where small groups of employees work together to improve their quality.

  Suppliers must also be encouraged to do all these things, so that they can give the best possible service. The success of Marks and Spencer has long been built upon the quality it demands from its suppliers.

- **Innovate** Always think of new ways of improving your products and the Seven Ss (see page 158). Small cross-functional groups can be very effective in achieving such innovation. People will also have to be as creative as possible, so have another look at Chapter Five. Every employee must think innovation, and the organisation must encourage it by rewarding new ideas with money and recognition.

- **Make it easy for customers to complain** It will make them happier if you deal with the complaints (whether justified or not) as quickly and effectively as possible. Think about a free telephone service for customers' suggestions and complaints.
- **Remember the lifetime value of your customers** When you provide a good service, they will come back to you. If a customer is spending £100 a week for ten years, this gives you a £50,000 customer. So treat him or her like one!
- **Prepare a Customer Charter** This should tell customers their rights, which you should make sure you honour.
- **Give a service guarantee** Offer customers their money back if they are not totally satisfied with your service. They will be impressed by this offer, and you won't have to pay anything because your service is so good.
- **Get your 5 Ps right** These are:

Price Important, particularly in relation to the quality of your product or service.

Place How you distribute and deliver your product or service to your customers, e.g. via retailers or mail order.

Product Customers are influenced not only by the physical characteristics of the product but also by their perceptions of it. For example, the marketing of Coca-Cola has made it not just a soft drink but also an 'experience' associated with a particular lifestyle. Think of the potential of your product or service to delight your customers and exceed their expectations.

Promotion How you promote or advertise your product or service.

People The service which your employees give to your customers before and after the sale of your product.

- *Educate your customers* Give them general background information related to your product or service, so that they can identify with it more. For example, Boots give out free health leaflets and the Body Shop issues literature on environmental issues.

- *Use information technology to respond more effectively to customer requirements than your competitors* For example, electronic point of sale systems (EPOS) mean that supermarkets know their sales figures by store and product within hours of closing.

- *Look after the little things* Small improvements in customer service can have a big impact on customers, e.g. McDonald's obsession with cleanliness. Particular attention to every little thing a customer might want is essential.

- *Learn faster than your competition* Learn from your mistakes as quickly as possible!

- *Don't let your customers wait too long* How quickly you can deliver is an important way to beat your competitors. Just think, for example, how quickly you can get a new pair of spectacles these days.

One Final Comment

The greatest management writer ever is probably the American Peter Drucker. He once wrote in his book, *The Practice of Management*, 'There is only one valid definition of business purpose: to create a customer.... It is the customer who determines what a business is.' Remember this.

SECTION C
How to Break Free and
Get Out of a Rut

13

LOVE YOUR WORK!

This chapter will show you how to:

▶ *Choose the career that will make you happy*

▶ *Interview better and sell yourself to the people you want to work for*

▶ *Get the qualifications and training you need to succeed*

▶ *Make your work fun and fulfilling*

THE Australian-born opera star, Dame Joan Sutherland, has had a wonderful life. She was lucky enough to be born with a great voice, but her self-discipline, emotional stability and placid nature have sustained her international success for over 40 years. Sutherland is happy because she chose and found the right career. Are you so lucky or are you in a rut and depressed or unhappy about your job? Do this quiz and you will find out:

Do You Love Mondays?

1 Do you look forward to Monday mornings on Sunday night?
2 Are you excited about your work?
3 Is your work like a hobby?
4 Are you optimistic about your future?
5 Can you relax at weekends and 'turn off' from your work?
6 Are you philosophical about your work problems?
7 Do you find some worthwhile purpose at work?
8 Do you have the support from others to help with your work problems?

The more you answer 'No' to these questions, the more you need to read this chapter! The first thing you must do is get on the right career track. After discussing this we will look at another vitally important issue: how to make your work fun and fulfilling.

How To Find The Right Career Track

● *Think about what you want from a job* Here is a list of things you might consider. Rank them in order of importance:

  a Financial security – having enough money to enjoy the lifestyle you want.
  b Autonomy – freedom to do what you like doing and be independent.
  c Managing people – dealing with organisational politics and the ability to delegate.
  d Responsibility – for other people's performance.
  e Achievement – doing something that you think is worthwhile.
  f Self-esteem – a feeling you are somebody with self-respect.

g Social contact – working and developing relationships with people.

h Work flexibility – working when you like, so that you can better satisfy the needs of your family and loved ones.

i Creativity – encouraging you to think of new ideas and giving you the opportunity to put them into action.

j Recognition – receiving reward and acclaim for your work.

k Outdoor activities – for people who don't like offices!

l Use of potential and expertise – employing your knowledge to good effect.

m Personal growth and development – a feeling you are developing your potential as a human being.

n Risk taking – taking chances and making speculative decisions.

o Status – the opportunity for promotion and a position with status.

p Variety – doing different things at work.

q Work/leisure balance – making sure you have enough time for your leisure and family.

Ask yourself: 'What is really important for me at work?' Does your work or family come first? Do you want less stress? Which career will achieve your personal goals in life? Remember these things before you make your next career move. If you want to set up your own business, turn to the next chapter for some advice.

● ***Know yourself***   Ask yourself: which career will use my strengths and minimise the impact of my weaknesses? A job which constantly reminds you of your deficiencies will be hell, even if it pays you a lot of money. So here is what you should do:

a List your strengths and weaknesses in order of importance – be honest! If you need some help in this, you might consider using one of the computer programmes such as Cascaid or Adult Direction. Ask about these at your local Careers Office.

b List the plus and minus points of your possible career, bearing in mind the things you might want from a career (see pages 165 and 166).

Compare the two lists. Which career is best suited to your strengths and weaknesses? Choose the career you want, not what other people think you ought to have. Remember it's your life, and during your lifetime you will spend over 75,000 hours at work!

- *Learn from career disappointments* Think of the reasons why a career was a failure for you, so that you don't make the same mistake again.

How To Grab Your Career Opportunities

JOB WINNER NO 1: KNOW THE JOBS MARKET

Once you have decided upon your chosen career, keep an eye on what jobs are available and which organisations are the best to work for. Read Bob Reynolds' book *The 100 Best Companies To Work For* (see Further Reading, page 202, for details).

JOB WINNER NO 2: DON'T STOP LEARNING

Re-read Chapter Four so that you can learn most effectively. But remember that learning is a lifelong experience. You must strive for continuous improvement and be constantly alive to what is happening around you, so that you can take advantage from it. If your career makes it difficult to do this, it's time to change your job! Alternatively, you might need some training.

JOB WINNER NO 3: GET THE QUALIFICATIONS AND TRAINING YOU NEED

Take every opportunity to learn from other people and develop your skills. Don't be afraid to get qualifications, if you consider them necessary to achieve your career goals. Talk to people about which qualifications may be best for you. For example, an MBA or completing your professional exams might be attractive. But whatever you do, bear in mind the following tips when you are studying:

- *Manage your time effectively* The quality of your study time is the most important thing.
- *Do coursework as soon as you receive it* This spreads your workload more evenly.
- *Be determined and keep reminding yourself of the benefits of successfully completing the course.*
- *Win the support of your family and loved ones* Think twice before doing a course if you have pre-school children. Remember someone has to look after them!
- *Improve your learning technique* (see Chapter Four).
- *Improve your examination technique by:*

  a reading the questions and instructions; answer the right number.

  b answering them directly and relevantly (remember you've probably only got 45 minutes to tell the examiner everything you know on the subject). Demonstrate a balance between quantity and quality in your answers and illustrate your answers with up-to-date examples.

  c avoiding difficult questions at the start of the exam, when you're nervous.

  d remembering you are at your most effective during the middle part of the exam.

  e writing clearly and legibly – remember examiners have a lot of papers to mark!

  f preparing yourself intellectually, physically and mentally for the exam; have concise notes so that you can learn key points in the syllabus. Practise doing past exam questions from memory in the time allocated and then see examiners' solutions. This is the best way to revise. Think positive, use slow deep breathing at times of stress and keep your body in good shape to give you energy to prepare for the exam. Eat sensibly, sleep well, and get lots of exercise to clear the mind! Arrive at the exam in plenty of time and find out beforehand where the exam room is located. Take a spare pen, any equipment (e.g. calculator) you'll need and chewing gum or sweets if they help you to relax.

g attempting all the questions; it is much easier to gain the first few marks for a question than the marks required to bring you up to distinction level. So plan your time and give yourself a strict time allocation for each question, based upon the marks given for it.

h sketching an outline plan for a question, but keep it very brief, as the plans won't be marked.

JOB WINNER NO 4: SELL YOURSELF EFFECTIVELY

Have another look at Chapters Nine and Ten. The ability to communicate well and influence people are obviously extremely important in improving your career prospects. First impressions can be particularly important. Have confidence in your abilities and don't sell yourself short.

JOB WINNER NO 5: WRITE A GOOD APPLICATION FORM

Look at the checklist below:

- **Think about your personal circumstances** The employer must be convinced that your age, family commitments and mobility won't stop you doing the job.
- **Complete the form in pencil first and then write over it** This saves making mistakes, but make sure you rub off any traces of pencil. You could also photocopy the form and practise filling it in. If you use a typewriter or

word processor, make sure you don't make mistakes! Be neat, and write clearly and precisely.

- *Remember that questions will be asked about your form at the interview* If you put mountaineering down as a hobby, and you've only done it once, you might not be able to give very informed answers on the subject. Be honest – if a lie is found out, you can say goodbye to the job unless there is a very good reason for your deceit.
- *Send the right form* If you are applying for lots of jobs, make sure you don't put the form in the wrong envelope.
- *Send your form on time* This tells the employer you are efficient and well organised.
- *Remember to photocopy it* This is important for your own reference.
- *Empathise with your potential employer* When you are writing the form, always be conscious of the type of person you think the employer wants for the job. Here are some things the employer may be looking for:

a Experience – academic and professional qualifications, training and experience.
b Communication skills.
c Ability to lead and influence others, considered by Marks and Spencer as the most important thing they look for from candidates for management posts.
d Manual dexterity.
e Physical fitness.
f Business acumen or commercial awareness.
g Suitability to be supervised.
h Creative ability.
i Problem solving ability.
j Ability to work alone.
k Skills to work well in a team.
l Ability to care for people.
m Self-motivation – the will to win and enthusiasm.
n Fluency in foreign language(s).

JOB WINNER NO 6: KNOW HOW TO WRITE A GOOD CV AND COVERING LETTER

A covering letter should be sent with the application form. It should say that you enclose your application form; you are grateful for the letter from the employer enclosing the application form; and you are available for interviews on a certain date. Be formal (i.e. Dear Sir (or Madam); Yours faithfully) with your name printed after your signature. The letter should be typed or very neatly written. Some organisations also ask for a CV (curriculum vitae). Ideally this should be typed on A4 paper, and be two pages maximum – brevity is important for impact! The author's CV is shown in Figure 1 (see page 177) to show what information should be included and how it should be structured. Here are some other tips about your CV:

- *It should be professionally typed* Looks are so important, so don't use a dot matrix printer with a word processor!
- *It should be perfect in grammar and spelling.*
- *Emphasise areas of specialist knowledge and experience.*
- *Avoid mention of interests and activities which might turn off some employers* (For example, politics and religion.)

For more information read Tom Jackson's book *The Perfect CV* (see Further Reading, page 202).

JOB WINNER NO 7: WRITE A SPECULATIVE LETTER

Even if a job has not been advertised it may be worth writing a speculative letter with your CV to an organisation you would like to work for. The aim of the letter is to arouse the interest of the reader and secure an interview, so emphasise why they should be interested in you (see Figure 2 on page 178).

JOB WINNER NO 8: INTERVIEW WELL

The job interview can make or break your career chances. So remember the 'dos and don'ts' of interviewing.

DO

- *Allow yourself plenty of time to arrive for the interview* Don't arrive flustered and late!
- *Look your best and project a professional image* First impressions count for a lot. Research shows that interviewers often make their decision in the first three or four minutes of the interview.
- *Keep yourself informed* Gather as much information as you can about the job and the organisation. If it is a company, look at its latest annual report.
- *Be positive and enthusiastic* Speak with clarity, confidence, conviction, enthusiasm and assertiveness. Practise this before the interview by playing your voice back on a tape recorder and learning from famous actors when they talk on book tapes. Just before you leave the interview, summarise why you're the best person for the job and thank the interviewer(s) for their interest.
- *Exude excellence in everything you say, write or do* Think positively and believe in yourself.
- *Think about what your potential employer wants.* (See page 170.)
- *Listen to the questions!*
- *Be honest.*
- *Make eye contact with your interviewer(s) and smile occasionally.*
- *Strike a balance between being too relaxed and too tense.*
- *Be personal and concise* Address your interviewer by name and keep your sentences short without omitting key issues.
- *Be prepared for small talk* Read the newspaper headlines on the day of the interview to give you material for social chit-chat at the beginning of the interview before the serious questioning begins.

- *Ask questions about the job* An important objective of the interview is to find out whether or not the job is right for you.
- *Prepare answers to questions the interviewer(s) might ask you.* For example:

Why do you want the job?

Why should I give the job to you?

Who has been the most influential person in your life and why?

Which is the most influential book you've read and why?

What has been the most satisfying experience in your life so far?

What are the characteristics of the best employer or teacher you have worked for?

What do you do to relax?

What positions of responsibility do you hold in your spare time?

What is the biggest problem you've had to overcome and how did you do it?

Why have you decided to leave your present job?

What are your ambitions for the future?

What has been your outstanding achievement in your last job?

How would you describe your present relationships with your colleagues and superiors?

How would you deal with difficult colleagues or superiors?

DON'T

- *Accept the job if it will make you unhappy.*
- *Forget copies of your CV and application form* These can remind you what you've said just before the interview.
- *Apply for jobs you have no intention of accepting.*
- *Be too critical about your last employers* The interviewer(s) might think you'll be a critical employee, too!
- *Be too casual or confident.*
- *Fidget* This distracts from what you are saying.
- *Be overawed by your interviewer(s)* They are human beings just like you!

- *Be aggressive or interrupt your interviewer(s).*
- *Annoy the interviewer(s) with your views*   A good rule of thumb is to be in favour of things rather than anti-anything. Don't volunteer your prejudices.
- *Say 'I want'*   Ask instead what you can do for the organisation and how you can improve yourself through, for example, training.
- *Talk about taboo subjects like sex, politics and religion.*
- *Give up all hope if you don't get the job*   Ask if there are any other opportunities within the organisation.

There are lots of good books on interviewing skills. It might be worthwhile buying one, or see Further Reading on p. 202.

JOB WINNER NO 9: NEVER GIVE UP

You might not achieve your career goals straightaway, but don't be put off if obstacles fall in your way. Be positive and determined to do the job that is best for you. Have a dream, and do everything you can to fulfil it. Find out all you can about the employer and the job before you apply. Use libraries, recruitment literature, annual reports, relevant periodicals and quality newspapers. University libraries will probably have McCarthy files, which are extremely useful because they gather together all newspaper cuttings relevant to a particular company.

How To Make Your Work Fun and Fulfilling

Shut your eyes for one moment and visualise yourself working in five years time. What are you doing? Are you in a rut, or have you a challenging and exciting career? The choice is yours. One thing is certain in today's job market: *you and nobody else is responsible for your career success and happiness.* The 'one job, one organisation' career is rapidly disappearing as companies cut back their workforces, sub-contract work and rely more on temporary and part-time staff. The trend towards flatter organisations with fewer levels of management is also making traditional career advancement up the hierarchy more difficult. So you will have to make sure that you will be a winner in the job market with the necessary specialist knowledge, self-motivation, self-confidence and ability to work in a team. Whatever you do, don't waste your future. Always have an answer to the question: 'What would I do if I lost my job tomorrow?' Go for that career which will make your future fun and exciting!

HOW YOU CAN MAKE YOUR CAREER EXCITING

The first two things to do we have discussed already: knowing yourself and lifelong learning. To make your work fun and fulfilling, you must also be very clear about what success really means to you. Promotion? Family and friends? Autonomy? Creativity? Recognition? Power and status? Money? Responsibility? Challenge? Variety? Peace of mind? Whatever you want, specify your goals clearly, so that you can do your best to achieve them at work.

The next thing you must do is think about what 'work' is. The best definition is *any productive activity*, so work can be both paid and unpaid. We all need financial security from our work, but your life will be more fulfilling if you serve people outside work. This is reflected in Charles Handy's idea of 'portfolio living' from his book *The Age of Unreason*. Such a life involves four areas of activity: paid work (your job); homework (children, cleaning etc.); gift work (done for free outside the home e.g. charity work); and study work (training and education). In short, fulfilment comes from a varied life.

To make the most of such a portfolio life, you must *value time not money*. Do you give yourself enough time for creativity, reflection, freedom of thought, and your family and friends? Effective time management can help you here, but however good you are at it, you can't create free time if your employer won't let you. If this is the case, it might be time for you to move to a less time-consuming job, even if it pays less money.

Finally you need to *take control of your life*. Only you can make your future at work fun and fulfilling. The responsibility is yours, so do something about your self-development! Be proactive, positive and assertive. Vehemently defend your right to be treated with humanity and respect, and learn to say no. Hold on to your dreams – set challenging but realistic goals for yourself. Take a leap in the dark by having the courage to do what you've always wanted to do but make sure you have carefully weighed up the pros and cons beforehand. Don't be impatient. It may be that you need to acquire further skills and confidence before you take the plunge. In these circumstances use your existing job as a springboard to the job of your dreams. Give yourself a break – take a holiday, or, if you can, a sabbatical. Critically reflect on your job and ask yourself: is it really what I want to do for the rest of my life?

You may have to change your attitudes to your present job,or change your job within your organisation. You may even have to leave it altogether and start something new. But whatever you do, never forget the words of Noel Coward: 'Work is much more fun than fun.' Do everything you can to make this true in your life.

One Final Thought

Do a career for the right reasons. American businessman and philosopher Benjamin Franklin once said his preferred epitaph was, 'I would rather have it said that "He lived usefully" than "He died rich".'

Name:	Philip Anthony Holden	
Date of Birth	29 September 1955	
Marital Status:	Married	
Home Address:	32 XYZ Street, Glasgow Tel:	
Work Address:	32 XYZ Street, Glasgow Tel:	
Education and Training:	1985	Graduate member of the IPM
	1984	MBA (City University, London)
	1977	Postgraduate Certificate in Education (London University)
	1976	BA Industrial Economics (Nottingham University)
Work Experience:	1988 to date	Lecturer in Business Policy, XYZ University, Glasgow
	1986–88	Lecturer in Business Policy, Portsmouth Polytechnic
	1978–86	Lecturer in Business Studies, Brooklands Technical College, Weybridge
	1977–78	Trainee Manager, Nationwide Building Society
Book Publications:	1996	Super Success (Piatkus)
	1989	BTEC Accounting (Heinemann)
	1987	BTEC Finance (Heinemann)
Other Interests:	Family, Gardening, Cooking and American History	
Referees:	Professor Smith, XYZ University Mr Brown, XYZ Company	

Figure 1: Curriculum Vitae

32, XYZ ST
GLASGOW
G3 0TB

6TH APRIL 199-

MR A BROWN
RECRUITMENT MANAGER
XYZ SUPERMARKET PLC
LONDON EC1

Dear Sir

I have just finished an MBA at Glasgow University, and I am looking for a job in supermarket management. I have five years experience in the food retailing industry, and during my MBA I completed a project on the future of supermarkets in the UK.

I feel that I have something to offer in the area of general management, marketing or human resources management.

I enclose my CV and shall look forward to hearing from you.

Yours faithfully

(Peter Green)

PETER GREEN

Figure 2: An Example of a Speculative Letter

14

GO IT ALONE - BE AN ENTREPRENEUR

This chapter will show you how to:

▶ *Decide whether or not self-employment is the right thing for you*

▶ *Run your own business*

ARE YOU IN A RUT? Do you want to break free and do your own thing? If so, this may be the right time to take the plunge and work for yourself. Such a move can be fraught with danger though, as for every business success there are hundreds of failures. The purpose of this chapter is to increase your chances of success by telling you the best way to run your own business. You could be a Richard Branson or Anita Roddick! They started with virtually nothing. Branson started trading from a telephone kiosk, and Roddick got off the ground with a £4,000 bank loan. They love their work not because they earn lots of money (although they wouldn't refuse it!) but because they are *living their lives their way*, leaving their personal imprints on the huge business empires they have created. Could you do the same?

Quiz: Could You Be a Richard Branson or Anita Roddick?

1 Are you passionate about achieving things in your life, and do you maintain this enthusiasm through the difficult periods?

2 Do you energetically pursue your goals and survive long hours?

3 Are you self-confident and determined when things go wrong?

4 Do you have a skill which could be sold to customers?

5 Can you control stress and make decisions when the going gets tough?

6 Are you good at selling yourself?

7 Do you know the difference between cash and profit?

8 Are you a good negotiator?

9 Are you prepared to take calculated risks?

10 Do you learn from other people and accept their good advice?

11 Will your family and loved ones totally support you in a new business venture?

12 Are you physically fit?

13 Have you the money to get started on your own?

14 Are you prepared to risk your house and possessions and suffer low pay for the sake of a new business?

15 Are you willing to give up your leisure time for your business?

16 Are you prepared to learn new skills for your business?

17 Do you think before you act?

18 Can you face the possibility of making decisions on your own?

19 Are you well organised, so that you do things in the quickest possible time?

20 Do you keep going until a task is as well done as it can be?

The more 'yes' answers you have (and be honest!) the more likely you are to become a successful entrepreneur. But it is obviously a big step to 'go it alone', so before you do anything, read the tips in this chapter about how to success-fully run a business. Think about the pros and cons of setting up your own business in terms of your career, finan-cial position and personal life, and the consequences of succeeding or failing in your business venture.

Remember that what counts is not fame or fortune but whether or not self-employment will make you a happier person. For example, you might not want to sacrifice time with your family and friends, but on the other hand self-employment may give you the freedom and fulfilment to make your time with your family even more rewarding. So be absolutely clear why you want to become self-employed. Write down as many reasons as you can why you would want to have a business of your own. Then make a list of the problems you might encounter. Compare the two lists – where do you stand in the self-employment stakes?

How To Run Your Own Business Successfully

You should have another look at Chapter Twelve, but here are some specific tips relating to new businesses:

KNOW YOURSELF

You must be absolutely clear about your reasons for setting up on your own. Your business venture is likely to be disas-trous if you're doing it for negative reasons, e.g. you hate your job. You can paint a better picture of self-employment than actually exists, and forget about the advantages of your job such as security and a regular income. So you may find yourself in a much worse position after you leave. You might yearn for your old 'boring' job when customers are not coming to your business, you haven't got the necessary skills, and the regular pay cheque isn't coming through every month! So do three things before you go it alone:

- **Be honest about your strengths and weaknesses**
Have you a skill or specialist knowledge that could be
sold to potential customers? Can you be confident
enough to succeed on your own? Can you take the
responsibility and the extra strain? If you are a sole trader
or in a partnership with unlimited liability for business
debts, can you face the possibility that your house and all
your possessions might have to be sold off if your business fails?

- **Set up on your own for positive reasons** Do it
because this is absolutely the right thing to do. Doing
anything new is a gamble to some extent, but reduce the
risks by making prior arrangements to deal with any
future problems associated with self-employment. For
example, if financial security is important to you, go into
a business where little capital is required and make sure
you have another income to fall back on, perhaps from
your savings or your partner's job. Then make a list of all
the positive reasons why you want to become an entrepreneur, such as: wanting to be rewarded adequately for your
own effort; a desire for independence (found by research
to be the main motivator for entrepreneurs – money isn't
so important!); fulfilling a dream (albeit a realistic one);
wanting to work at home (you may want to see more of
your family and reduce your travelling time); and a desire
to be creative.

- **Put your business in perspective** Ask yourself: if the
business failed, would it be the end of your life? Surely
not! The people in your life must be more important. So
view a business failure philosophically and don't get
carried away when you're successful. 'Remain level-
headed', Alan Sugar, founder of Amstrad, has said, 'and
realise that as quickly as you can rise to fame, you can fall
twice as fast'. This is not to say that you should expect
failure – far from it. It is essential to earn an adequate
living from your business, so ask yourself the question: is
there a big enough market for your proposed product or
service?

PREPARE A BUSINESS PLAN

A business plan is essential not only for the successful running of a business but also for banks, if you want to borrow money. It shows what the business will be hoping to do in the future in the following areas:

- **Mission**   This is a statement of your business's objectives in one sentence, for example, 'to be the best firm by delighting and exceeding the expectations of our customers'.
- **Market information**   Who are your customers? Is your market growing or getting smaller? What are the prices, strengths and weaknesses of your competitors? Can you keep pace with the level of innovation introduced by your competitors? Have you done any market research? Will your product or service be promoted and packaged effectively?
- **Production information**   What are your products or services, including their proposed price? Have you taken into account all your expenses when calculating your price? How effective will your production and purchasing be? Will there be any problems with plant, machinery, equipment and vehicles?
- **Financial information**   (see pages 189 to 191) What is your expected turnover in your first year and the annual percentage change in turnover in the first five years? What is your break-even figure? What assets can you use as security for a loan (if required)? How much money do you need and where will you get it from? Will you have enough cash to pay your annual expenses? Will your profits rise as a proportion of turnover in your first five years?
- **Business premises**   If freehold, what is the valuation of the property and its size? If leasehold, what are the main terms of the lease, such as who is responsible for maintenance and repairs? Will the premises be big enough for your present and future needs? Are they located in the best possible place?
- **Key personnel (including yourself)**   What experience, qualifications and knowledge do they have?

The reasons for preparing a business plan are to make you think ahead and anticipate any future problems, and exploit any future business opportunities.

BE AN INSPIRATIONAL LEADER

A successful business person must inspire people to do great things, whether they are employees or people outside the business such as suppliers and customers. What was said in Chapters Ten and Eleven are just as relevant to entrepreneurs as they are to everybody else. But there are several particular points you should remember, if you are to set up your own business:

- *Choose work you love to do* It's hard to be inspirational when you hate what you're doing.
- *Remember there is nobody else to give the business leadership* Unlike in other jobs there is nobody else to rely on. So accept the responsibility to give your business a mission and a sense of purpose. If anyone works for you, they should clearly understand what the objectives of your business are. Communicate passion, enthusiasm and excitement about what you are trying to do in the business.
- *Never look worried* There will be anxious and stressful times when you are out on your own. But as soon as you start to show it, people will lose faith and confidence in you. So look confident and believe in your ability to overcome any obstacles or difficulties in your way.
- *Take calculated risks* The successful entrepreneur is a risk taker, but he does it with caution. For example, one of Richard Branson's golden rules of management has always been to 'limit the downside'. He seizes any potentially profitable opportunities, but he makes sure that if they fail they don't bring the whole of his business down as well. So he purposely kept his airline relatively small, and in the first year of its operations, leased only one 747 from Boeing on the condition they could take it back if things didn't work out.
- *Empower people* If you believe someone has a good idea, give them the resources and autonomy to success-

fully implement it. Value people because of their ability not because of their status or position.

● *Give your undivided attention to the people that matter* Prioritise, but once you've decided that something is important, give it everything you've got and show that concern to other people. Be well organised (good filing systems, effective time management, etc.), so that your help for others is as effective as possible.

BE SELF-MOTIVATED AND DETERMINED

There is no short cut to business success – you never get anything for nothing! You will have to maintain your self-motivation to succeed. Of course, that is much easier if you really enjoy what you are doing. For example, Anita Roddick emphasises the importance of having a sense of 'joy, magic and fun'. It is also important to set ambitious but realistic goals for yourself. Victor Kiam of Remington razors' fame believes that the successful entrepreneur must find a motivator other than money. Both Roddick and Branson agree – they see money as a means to be more creative and fulfilled, not the be all and end all. Be persistent in pursuit of your goals, and never take no for an answer. If a door slams in your face, beat it down!

BE LUCKY!

Take full advantage of any luck that might come your way, and work hard to make your own luck.

SEEK AND FIND HELP AND SUPPORT

Your business will require total dedication, but it's not worth it if your family and loved ones suffer as a consequence. So make the best possible use of your time to make time for the people you love (see Chapter Six). This will not only give you a happier life but also help your business. If your family think your business comes before them you will lose their support, which is vital in times of anxiety and stress. Extra leisure time also re-charges your mental abilities so that you can tackle your business problems with greater skill and enthusiasm.

Make sure you have a good solicitor, accountant (to help with your tax returns and accounts) and bank manager. Rely on their advice, but have any relevant information at your fingertips, so that you can ask them the right questions and keep them on their toes. So pay special attention to what is written in this chapter. Another very useful source of advice is your local enterprise agency – see the Yellow Pages for the telephone number, or ring Business in the Community (0171 629 1600).

You will also need advice about your personal finances from an independent financial adviser. When you become self-employed you will lose fringe benefits like a company pension and sick pay. It is vital that you take out a personal pension plan and insurance against sickness.

STAY HEALTHY, ENERGETIC AND STRESS-FREE

What was said in Chapters Seven and Eight is particularly relevant if you are self-employed. If you are sick there's nobody to cover for you, and you stop earning! Self-employment has a worry around every corner, so make sure you control stress. You will need to work long hours, where necessary. Energy and stamina are essential for business success.

HAVE THE CONFIDENCE TO BELIEVE IN YOURSELF

Believe in what you are trying to do in your business. Identify with its purpose. This will give you the confidence to cope with any problems. Be positive!

LOVE YOUR CUSTOMERS

Customer satisfaction is the only thing that will make your business a winner. So provide a quality product or service, innovate, find a gap in the market and keep in touch with what the customer wants through market research. If your business grows, you will need the support of a committed workforce. Don't forget that happy employees mean happy customers. Every employee in every department must be totally dedicated to customer satisfaction. Flexibility, service and speed of response to customers' requirements are the three main reasons why smaller firms can beat bigger competitors. Think of all the successful small businesses in your area, and you will see why.

KNOW YOUR COMPETITION

Know your competitors' strengths and weaknesses. Avoid their strengths and take advantage of their weaknesses. Try to anticipate how they will react to changes in your policies, so that you can plan to do something about them.

HAVE ENOUGH RESOURCES OF THE RIGHT QUALITY

The 'Four Ms' remind you of the resources you will need in your business:

- *Men (and women!)*   Recruit the best people and give them the best possible training.
- *Money*   See below.
- *Materials*   Get the best possible deal from your suppliers.
- *Machinery (and land)*   Use them to achieve your business objectives. Remember machinery and computers have to be used appropriately and effectively to boost your profits. If land is scarce, you may have to relocate your business. Your most precious resource of all is your time, though, so use it well and get organised!

LOCATE IN THE RIGHT PLACE

Where your business operates from is dependent upon several factors:

- **Your own objectives** Locate to reduce travelling time and also where there are good schools for your children and a job for your partner. Alternatively, if you can, you may want to work at home to see more of your family.
- **Recruitment** If you need employees you will have to be in an area where there are people with the right skills.
- **Government regional grants** The government provides financial help to businesses in areas of high unemployment. For example, firms in enterprise zones don't have to pay council tax for five years (applicable at time of going to press). Contact your local enterprise agency (see Yellow Pages), to see if your business might be eligible for government assistance.
- **Your market** Your business must be conveniently situated for your customers. Good access to motorways, or another suitable form of transport may be essential to get your products to your customers as quickly as possible. This will also help your suppliers to get goods to you.

BE PERSUASIVE AND KNOWLEDGEABLE

Communicate well and influence people (see Chapters Nine and Ten). Improve your selling and negotiating skills, and bear in mind that knowledge is the passport to business success. Make sure you have specialist knowledge which makes customers do business with you. Continuously learn to improve your service to your customers.

MANAGE YOUR MONEY WELL

You must have knowledge of accountancy, if you are to run your business well. So here are some tips your accountant might give you:

TIP 1: KNOW YOUR BALANCE SHEET AND PROFIT AND LOSS ACCOUNT

Your balance sheet is a 'snapshot' of your business's financial position on a particular day, showing you how well (or how badly) off you are. It is a statement of your assets, liabilities and capital on that particular day.

a **Assets** can be either fixed or current. **Fixed assets** are used for a long time (eg. premises, machinery and vehicles) and depreciation is normally deducted from their value. **Current assets** are either cash or convertible into cash within one year of the date of the balance sheet (e.g. bank balance, stocks, and debtors – customers who haven't paid you yet).

b **Liabilities** refer to money you owe other people. They can be **current liabilities** which have to be repaid to your creditors within one year of the date of the balance sheet (e.g. suppliers you haven't paid yet) or **longer term liabilities** such as bank loans.

c **Capital** is the amount you and other people have put into the business.

Your business's profit and loss account should include, for your accounting year, all your business's income (your sales revenue or **turnover**) and all its expenditures, except any spending on fixed assets. Obviously your income less your expenditures is your **profit**.

TIP 2: MAKE SURE YOU HAVE ENOUGH CASH

Remember profit isn't the same thing as cash. Some of your customers may buy on credit. So a sale will be entered into your accounts without you receiving any cash for it. Ways of giving your business more cash are:

- *Yourself* The more you contribute the greater the risk to you, however.
- *Bank loan and overdrafts* You may need security like your house or life assurance policy, though. Also note your ability to pay the loan repayments and interest.
- *Boosting the number of cash customers* Do this

through a good product or service and effective sales and marketing.

- **Credit control** Make sure your debtors pay up on time through reminder letters and, if necessary, a letter from your solicitor.
- **Stock control** Keeping your stock levels as low as possible without reducing the effectiveness of your business makes sense.
- **Completing a cash flow forecast** This outlines your planned cash payments and cash receipts month by month, and will show when you are likely to be short of cash so that you can do something about it.
- **Delaying payment for assets** Do this through leasing or hire-purchase.
- **Selling fixed assets** This may be considered as a last resort measure but sale and lease back has become quite common, where you sell an asset to a leasing company and then lease it back.
- **Factoring** This is when you sell your debts to a finance company which then collects them. You will, of course, lose a considerable percentage of the money.
- **Delaying payment as long as you can** Richard Branson has said that the phrase which kept his company alive in the early years was 'the cheque is in the post'.
- **Making sure you don't grow too fast** The extra borrowing needed to do this may cripple your business.
- **Find out if you are eligible for financial help from the government** Contact your local enterprise agency about this.

TIP 3: CONTROL YOUR COSTS

Controlling costs is obviously vital to keep profits up and to sell your product or service at a reasonable price. Remember that the most common method of pricing is cost plus pricing – that is, costs per unit + mark-up (profit) = price. There are two types of costs you will have to watch:

- **Fixed costs** Spending on fixed assets which doesn't immediately change when you increase your production or sales.

- *Variable costs* Costs which vary with production and sales, such as overtime and materials bought.

The best way to control costs is to use monthly budgets which show your planned expenditure for each month. Then you must compare what you *actually* spend with what you *planned* to spend. Clearly, if your actual spending is greater then you'll have to control your costs.

TIP 4: MEASURE THE PERFORMANCE OF YOUR BUSINESS

There are some useful ways to check how well your business is doing:

- Profit margin:

$$\frac{profit}{sales} \times 100\%$$

- Profit as a percentage of your capital:

$$\frac{profit}{\text{Total assets less current liabilities}} \times 100\%$$

- Break-even point (i.e. the numbers of units you will have to produce or sell before you start to make a profit):

$$\frac{\text{fixed costs } (£)}{\text{selling price } (£) \text{ less variable costs per unit } (£)}$$

TIP 5: KNOW ABOUT BOOK-KEEPING

You will have to decide whether or not you are going to do your own books, or employ an accountant. A book-keeping course will save you a lot of money. You will need to learn to complete essential documents like your:

- *Cash book* This includes all items of cash income and expenditure.
- *Sales book* This states all credit sales where customers don't pay immediately.
- *Purchases book* Entries in this book are all credit purchases where you don't pay your suppliers immediately.
- *VAT return* Applicable only if you pay VAT. It lists the value of all goods or services sold by your business.

One Final Thought

Remember you have only one life. So if you are right for self-employment, go for it! It is so easy to settle into a secure rut when what your life really needs is something new and challenging. Do make absolutely sure that your new business stands a good chance of success, however. There are lots of extremely happy self-employed people, but there are also many others who have lost their self-esteem by failing in a new business. Do your homework, and remember what is in this chapter!

15

THE SECRETS OF SUCCESS

WELL DONE, you've nearly made it to the end of the book! But how far down the road are you to fulfilling your true potential? Of course it isn't easy, but when you are there, the prize is beyond measure: a happy and useful life. Go for it and put a smile on your face! Be a winner not only in your job but also in your personal life. To do this you must remind yourself of the recurrent themes of the book.

Fulfilment

This book has continually tried to get you to think about your definition of success and your purpose in life. These are the essential prerequisites of making the most of your potential. One message should have come out clearly: *success is more than performing well in your job*. It is about striking the right balance between your job and your personal life; generating passion, enthusiasm and excitement in your life; and finding the right values and peace of mind. The saddest paradox of our modern age is that progress means less time for the people who really matter. Any civilised society should be judged on the quality of its social relationships, not on its affluence.

Material success should, therefore, be a means to an end. It should enable you to discover your soul and spiritual fulfilment. Don't be enslaved by your job and the money it brings, but use them to improve the quality of your life. At the end of the get-rich-quick 1980s, a study in the USA found that nearly half of the men studied felt that their lives were empty and meaningless, despite years of trying to attain professional success. Fill that moral vacuum by digging into your soul and improving yourself from within. Remember the words of Thomas Jefferson, that happiness is 'tranquillity, occupation, knowledge, and a virtuous life'. If you forget that advice, your very life could be at stake. Research shows that people with unhappy social relationships are more likely to die early.

Sir Edmund Hillary, the New Zealander who conquered Everest, won fame, but it was not enough for him. In his autobiography, *Nothing Venture, Nothing Win*, he looks at his life with great dissatisfaction, because he could have done so much more with it. What really matters, he says, is 'not just achieving things ... but the advantage you have taken of your opportunities and the opportunities you created.' Climbing Everest was not the pinnacle of his life. What made him happiest was his relationships with the people he loved. If you recognise the truth of this philosophy, you will be on top of the world, too!

Love

Self-improvement without love is like a life without breath. Empathy, cheerful giving, friendship, and a sense of community are all essential to a happy and successful life. Live to love and the whole world will smile with you!

Courage

You must have the moral courage and confidence to do what's right in your life. Face up to yourself. Honestly assess your strengths and weaknesses, however painful that may prove to be. Deal with other people assertively, and win respect by defending your rights. Stand up and be counted. You take a risk in putting your head above the parapet, but this is better and more challenging than hiding your head in the sand! Follow the advice of the psychologist, Erich Fromm, *have the courage to be human.*

Freedom

Freedom is a mercurial goal, but it's worth striving for. A central message of this book has been to do your own thing within the constraints of having to earn a living. Seek autonomy, work flexibility, freedom of thought and creativity from your job. Throw off your chains and experience the spiritual liberation that only true freedom can bring!

Fun

Your life should be fun, exciting and happy, so seek work that you love, stay healthy, have a good laugh and put time and effort into your relationships with others.

Hope

A useful life is full of hope and optimism, so always be positive, and conquer your fears and anxieties.

Lifelong Learning

Successful people never stop learning, listening and striving to be creative. In this sense the quest for self-improvement is continuous – a race without a finish line.

Self-marketing

Think of everybody you meet as a customer, and do your best to satisfy their needs and wants. Delight them and exceed their expectations! Sell yourself through effectively communicating and empathising with them.

Some Final Comments

If you want to transform your life, you must completely rethink the way you live it. Define your purpose in life, and ensure that you achieve it. You may have to make compromises, but in the end your will to win will see you through to a happier, more fulfilled life. Success through self-improvement is an attitude of mind. Change your attitudes and you will change yourself.

QUIZ ANSWERS

ANSWERS TO QUIZ ON INVENTORS AND DISCOVERERS, CHAPTER FIVE

Aeroplane – The Wright Brothers
Car – Karl Benz
Camera – George Eastman
Electric light bulb – Thomas Edison
Telephone – Alexander Graham Bell
Telescope – Galileo
Television – John Logie Baird
Pneumatic tyre – John Dunlop
Penicillin – Alexander Fleming
Radio signals – Marconi
Radium – Marie and Pierre Curie

ANALYSIS, CHAPTER FIVE

Give yourself two points for a 'Yes' answer, nothing for a 'No' in questions 1 to 10. The possible answers to questions 11–14 are:

11 Wrapping a present, drawing on it, making paper decorations, lighting a fire, covering a shelf.
12 Look at a dictionary!
13 Marshmallows, chocolates, dumplings, brussels sprouts, oranges.
14 Lion, tiger, monkey, zebra, gorilla, snake, antelope, elephant, hippopotamus, rhinoceros.

Give yourself one point for each correct answer.

Over 45 You are highly creative, but do you know why? Read this chapter and find out!

25–45   You are creative in some ways, but certain areas need improving.

Under 25 You need to take a serious look at how to be more creative.

ANALYSIS, CHAPTER ELEVEN

Give yourself two points for each 'Yes' answer. Nothing for a 'No'.

Over 80   You really are a great manager but do you know why?

50–79   You have many qualities as a manager but there is room for improvement.

Under 50 You still have much to learn!

Now check your answers under the following headings to see where you can improve your performance:

1	Are you visible?
2–4	Do you have a vision and can you motivate people to work for it?
5	Are your people's objectives clearly laid down?
6–10	Are you prepared to learn?
11–27	Do you empower your people?
28–32	Do you set standards of excellence?
33–36	Do you lead by example?
37	Do you stand by your employees?
38	Have you the ability to manage?
39–40	Do you treat people equally?
41	Do you get the work/leisure balance right?
42–44	Do you do what you think is right?

SUGGESTED FURTHER READING

HOW TO MAKE THE MOST OF YOURSELF

Michael Argyle, *Psychology of Happiness* (Methuen, 1987)
  An excellent book on what makes you happy.
Jacqueline Atkinson, *Coping with Stress at Work* (Thorsons, 1988)
  The best introductory book I've seen on stress.
Bible
  Whether you are a Christian or not, the Bible contains a wealth
  of wisdom. Particularly reflect on Romans 12; 1 Corinthians 12;
  and James 1.
Tony Buzan, *Make the Most of Your Mind* (Pan, 1988)
  How to excel through your mind, by Britain's leading expert on
  the subject.
Dale Carnegie, *How to Win Friends and Influence People* (Cedar,
  1988)
  Still a classic.
Stephen R. Covey, *Daily Reflections for Highly Effective People*
  (Fireside, 1994)
  A good summary of his highly influential best seller, The Seven
  Habits of Highly Effective People.
P. Evans and F. Bartolomé, *Must Success Cost So Much?* (Basic
  Books, 1981)
  Valuable research on the price of success.
Michael Eysenck, *Happiness* (Erlbaum, 1990)
  Another excellent book on happiness.
Gerald Hargreaves, Dorothy Morfett, Geraldine Bown, *Making
  Time* (BBC, 1993)
  The best introductory book I've seen on time management.
Gael Lindenfield, *Assert Yourself* (Thorsons, 1992)

A good introduction to assertiveness.
Barry Lynch, *BBC Health Check* (BBC, 1989)
A very good introductory book on health.
Bryan Magee, *The Great Philosophers* (Oxford University Press, 1987)
The best introduction to philosophy I've seen.
Mark McCormack, *What They Don't Teach You at Harvard Business School* (Collins, 1984)
Best seller with some useful tips for success.
Ann McGhee-Cooper, *You Don't Have To Go Home from Work Exhausted* (Bowen & Rodgers, 1990)
Some useful tips about how to become more energetic.
Norman Vincent Peale, *The Power of Positive Thinking* (Heinemann, 1952)
Extremely influential book.
M. Scott Peck, *The Road Less Travelled* (Walker & Co, 1985)
A thought-provoking book about how to achieve success through spiritual fulfilment. Hugely successful in America.
Reader's Digest Magazine.
Well worth reading. Concise and informative.
Anthony Robbins, *Unlimited Power* (Simon and Schuster, 1988)
Another interesting self-improvement book.

Useful articles on making the most of yourself are:

L. Bongiorno, 'The B-School Profs At The Head of Their Class' (*Business Week*, 28 October 1994)
B. Darrack, 'Dreams and Passions of Meryl Streep' (Reader's Digest, April 1988)
K. L. Johnson, 'Desperation and Successful Men' (*Broker World*, November 1989)
G. Perret, 'How To Get A Laugh' (*Reader's Digest*, February, 1992)
L. Smith, 'Stamina: Who Has It, Why You Need It, How You Get It' (*Fortune*, 28 November 1994)
'Time Management' (Factsheet 36, *Personnel Management*, December 1990)
S. Toksvig, 'Look Who's Talking' (*Good Housekeeping*, January 1994)

BIOGRAPHIES AND AUTOBIOGRAPHIES

Read as many as you can to learn from other people's experiences.
Here is a selection I have found useful:

M. Bragg, *Rich* (Hodder & Stoughton, 1988) – Richard Burton

S. Bramley, *Leonardo: The Artist and the Man* (Michael Joseph, 1992)

R. W. Clark, *Edison, The Man who Made the Future* (Macdonald & Jane's, 1977)

R. W. Clark, *Einstein, The Life and Times* (Hodder & Stoughton, 1973)

D. Fingleton, *Kiri* (Collins, 1982)

C. Flippo, *McCartney, The Biography* (Sidgwick & Jackson, 1988)

F. Freidel, *Franklin D. Roosevelt: A Rendezvous With Destiny* (Little, Brown, 1990)

D. J. Garrow, *Bearing The Cross* (Vintage, 1993) – Martin Luther King

B. Geldof, *Is That It?* (Penguin, 1986)

M. Gilbert, *Churchill, A Life* (Mandarin, 1993)

N. Hamilton, *Monty: The Man Behind the Legend* (Sphere, 1987)

E. Hillary, *Nothing Venture, Nothing Win* (Hodder and Stoughton, 1975)

V. Kiam, *Going For It!* (Collins, 1986)

E. Lax, *Woody Allen* (Jonathan Cape, 1991)

N. Major, *Joan Sutherland* (Little, Brown, 1987)

N. Mandela, *Long Walk to Freedom* (Little, Brown, 1995)

A. Roddick & R. Miller, *Body and Soul* (Ebury Press, 1991)

I. Rosenwater, *Sir Donald Bradman* (Batsford, 1978)

N. Schwarzkopf & P. Petre, *It Doesn't Take a Hero* (Bantam, 1992).

D. Shipman, *Marlon Brando* (Sphere, 1989)

B. P. Thomas, *Abraham Lincoln* (Eyre & Spottiswoode, 1953)

A. Walker, *Elizabeth* (Weidenfeld & Nicolson, 1990) – Elizabeth Taylor

T. J. Watson & P. Petre, *Father Son and Co, My Life at IBM and Beyond* (Bantam, 1990)

M. White & J. Gribbin, *Stephen Hawking: A Life in Science* (Viking, 1992)

HOW TO DEAL WITH PEOPLE AT WORK

Warren Bennis and Burt Nanus, *Leaders* (Harper & Row, 1985)
Influential book on characteristics of successful American chief executives.

Philippa Davies, *Your Total Image – How To Communicate Success* (Piatkus, 1994)
Useful on communication skills.

Max Eggert, *The Perfect Interview* (Century, 1992)
  A very good book on how to interview well.
John Harvey-Jones, *Making it Happen* (Collins, 1987)
  How to be a good leader, by the former boss of ICI.
Robert Heller, *The Supermanagers* (Sidgwick and Jackson, 1984)
  Another useful guide to successful management.
Jane Lyle, *Understanding Body Language* (Chancellor Press, 1993)
  Excellent on interpreting body language.
Fred Orr, *How To Succeed at Work* (Unwin, 1987)
  A great little book.
Tom Peters & Robert Waterman, *In Search of Excellence* (Harper & Row, 1982)
  Still the best introduction to how organisations should be run.
Warren Smith, *Managing From The Heart* (Executive Excellence, November 1991)
  Useful article on management.
Martin John Yate, *Great Answers to Tough Interview Questions* (Kogan Page, 1992)
  Another excellent book on interviewing skills.

HOW TO BREAK FREE AND GET OUT OF A RUT

Charles Handy, *Age of Unreason* (Arrow, 1990)
Charles Handy, *The Empty Raincoat* (Hutchinson, 1994)
  Two fascinating books on the future of work from the great man himself.
Tom Jackson, *The Perfect CV* (Piatkus, 1991)
  A good book on how to get the job you really want.
Gary Jones, *Starting Up* (Pitman, 1988)
  Essential reading, if you want to set up your own business.
Bob Reynolds, *The 100 Best Companies to Work For* (Collins Fontana, 1989)
  The best of British employers, with useful things to look for in a job.
Alan West, *A Business Plan* (Pitman, 1988)
  An important book, if you want to set up your own business.

COURSES

One day training courses are a very valuable way of learning how to maximise the potential of yourself and your employees. The author of this book, Philip Holden, is available for one day seminars and in-company training. For further details, please contact:

Philip Holden,
P.O. Box 27,
Midhurst,
West Sussex
GU29 9YE.

ABOUT THE AUTHOR

Philip Holden is currently working as a lecturer in business policy at Glasgow Caledonian University. He is a lecturer of seventeen years' standing, with expert experience of running MBA and undergraduate courses and seminars relating to the issues covered in this book.

He has written two accountancy textbooks, *BTEC Finance* and *BTEC Accounting*, both published by Heinemann.

Philip received his BA from Nottingham University in 1976, and his Postgraduate Certificate in Teaching from London University in 1977. He also received his MBA from City University, London, in 1984. Membership of the British Institute of Personnel Management followed a year later. He currently lives in Glasgow, Scotland, with his wife and two daughters.

Philip Holden is available for one day seminars and in-company training. For further details, please contact:

Philip Holden, PO Box 27, Midhurst, West Sussex GU29 9YE.

Piatkus Business Books

Piatkus Business Books have been created for people who need expert knowledge readily available in a clear and easy-to-follow format. All the books are written by specialists in their field. They will help you improve your skills quickly and effortlessly in the workplace and on a personal level.

Titles include:

General Management and Business Skills

Be Your Own PR Expert: the complete guide to publicity and public relations   Bill Penn
Complete Conference Organiser's Handbook, The   Robin O'Connor
Complete Time Management System, The   Christian H Godefroy and John Clark
Confident Decision Making   J Edward Russo and Paul J H Schoemaker
Corporate Culture   Charles Hampden-Turner
Energy Factor, The: how to motivate your workforce   Art McNeil
Firing On All Cylinders: the quality management system for high-powered corporate performance   Jim Clemmer with Barry Sheehy
How to Implement Change in Your Company   John Spencer and Adrian Pruss
Influential Manager, The: How to develop a powerful management style   Lee Bryce
Influential Woman, The: How to achieve success in your career – and still enjoy your personal life   Lee Bryce
Leadership Skills for Every Manager   Jim Clemmer and Art McNeil
Lure the Tiger Out of the Mountains: timeless tactics from the East for today's successful manager   Gao Yuan
Managing For Performance   Alasdair White
Managing Your Team   John Spencer and Adrian Pruss
Outstanding Negotiator, The   Christian H Godefroy and Luis Robert
Problem Solving Techniques That Really Work   Malcolm Bird
Right Brain Time Manager, The   Dr Harry Alder
Seven Cultures of Capitalism, The: value systems for creating wealth in Britain, the United States, Germany, France, Japan,

Getting What You Want Quentin de la Bedoyere
Memory Booster: easy techniques for rapid learning and a better memory Robert W Finkel
Napoleon Hill's Keys to Success Matthew Sartwell (ed.)
Napoleon Hill's Unlimited Success Matthew Sartwell (ed.)
NLP: The New Art and Science of Getting What You Want Dr Harry Alder
Organise Yourself Ronni Eisenberg and Kate Kelly
Personal Growth Handbook, The Liz Hodgkinson
Personal Power Philippa Davies
Quantum Learning: unleash the genius within you Bobbi DePorter with Mike Hernacki
Right Brain Manager, The: how to use the power of your mind to achieve personal and professional success Dr Harry Alder
10-Minute Time and Stress Management Dr David Lewis
Three Minute Meditator, The David Harp with Nina Feldman
Total Confidence Philippa Davies

Sales and Customer Services

Art of the Hard Sell, The Robert L Shook
Commonsense Marketing For Non-Marketers Alison Baverstock
Creating Customers David H Bangs
Guerrilla Marketing Excellence Jay Conrad Levinson
Guerrilla Marketing Jay Conrad Levinson
Guerrilla Marketing On The Internet Jay Conrad Levinson and Charles Rubin
How Close Every Sale Joe Girard
How to Make Your Fortune Through Network Marketing John Bremner
How to Succeed in Network Marketing Leonard Hawkins
How to Win a Lot More Business in a Lot Less Time Michael LeBoeuf
How to Win Customers and Keep Them for Life Michael LeBoeuf
How to Write Letters that Sell Christian Godefroy and Dominique Glocheux
One-to-One Future, The Don Peppers and Martha Rogers
Sales Power: the Silva mind method for sales professionals José Silva and Ed Bernd Jr
Selling Edge, The Patrick Forsyth
Telephone Selling Techniques That Really Work Bill Good
Winning New Business: a practical guide to successful sales presentations Dr David Lewis

Presentation and Communication

Better Business Writing Maryann V Piotrowski

Complete Book of Business Etiquette, The   Lynne Brennan and David Block

Confident Conversation   Dr Lillian Glass

Confident Speaking: how to communicate effectively using the Power Talk System   Christian H Godefroy and Stephanie Barrat

He Says, She Says: closing the communication gap between the sexes   Dr Lillian Glass

Personal Power   Philippa Davies

Powerspeak: the complete guide to public speaking and presentation   Dorothy Leeds

Presenting Yourself: a personal image guide for men   Mary Spillane

Presenting Yourself: a personal image guide for women   Mary Spillane

Say What You Mean and Get What You Want   George R. Walther

Your Total Image   Philippa Davies

Careers and Training

How to Find the Perfect Job   Tom Jackson

Jobs for The Over 50s   Linda Greenbury

Making It As A Radio Or TV Presenter   Peter Baker

Marketing Yourself: how to sell yourself and get the jobs you've always wanted   Dorothy Leeds

Networking and Mentoring: a woman's guide   Dr Lily M Segerman-Peck

Perfect CV, The   Tom Jackson

Perfect Job Search Strategies   Tom Jackson

Secrets of Successful Interviews   Dorothy Leeds

Sharkproof: get the job you want, keep the job you love in today's tough job market   Harvey Mackay

10-Day MBA, The   Steven Silbiger

Ten Steps To The Top   Marie Jennings

Which Way Now? – how to plan and develop a successful career   Bridget Wright

For a free brochure with further information on our complete range of business titles, please write to:

Piatkus Books
Freepost 7 (WD 4505)
London W1E 4EZ

PIATKUS